D0544231

The
Television Researcher's
Guide

Kathy Chater

 **BBC** *Television Training*

First published in 1989 by
BBC Television Training
BBC Elstree Centre
Clarendon Road
Borehamwood
Hertfordshire

Revised edition 1992
© BBC Television Training
All rights reserved
ISBN 0 948694 80 7

A CIP catalogue record
for this book is available from
The British Library

General Editor:
Gordon Croton

Design and production:
Shirley Greenfield

Printed by
BBC Print Unit
Evesham
England

CONTENTS:

FOREWORD

Naturally I think that, as a researcher, I've got the best job in television. I meet a lot of interesting people and learn numerous interesting facts that can paralyse a dinner party. There is no other job that brings so much contact with an infinitely wide range of people and subject matter.

I have worked in almost every production department in the BBC and done most kinds of research. I have checked answers to quiz questions, tracked down clips of archive film, looked for people to illustrate proposed changes in the law, found subjects for documentary films, made a list of sources for a proposed biography of an actor and a thousand and one other tasks which have come under the heading of 'research'. No single book could hope to cover everything that a researcher might be asked to find out or do.

Those who are already researchers may laugh hollowly at much of the advice that follows and I have to admit that a great deal of it is the counsel of perfection; what would be done given the ideal amount of time and resources.

One of the great benefits of working for such a large organisation as the BBC is the number of support services: departments dealing with problems of copyright, artists contracts, the law — as well as offices overseas which can help with foreign matters. We are also lucky to have a library service, a news information service and an extensive network of gramophone and music libraries covering everything from pop to plainsong. In this handbook, I have tried to list as many outside sources as I can for those who aren't so pampered.

Almost everyone I have ever worked with has taught me something new about research and programme making and it would take too long, as well as sounding like one of the more interminable Oscar-winner's speeches, to list them all. I am indebted to a number of people, both inside and outside the BBC, who have let me pick their brains for the price of a drink.

A lot of people are going to disagree with my methods and conclusions. All I can say is they've worked all right for me so far. Experienced researchers may also find the advice about how to find people, facts, etc. boringly basic, but I have tried to include as many useful addresses and telephone numbers as I can. As these are the backbone of every researcher's work, there should be something here for everyone.

KATHY CHATER

Chapter 1

What is Research?

Part I

This is one of those 'How long is a piece of string?' questions. In television, research covers a wide range of tasks of various degrees of complexity from checking the answers to general knowledge questions for a quiz show to finding film and original factual material for a thirteen-part documentary series. There are also research posts which involve selecting people to appear on programmes as contestants, as chat show guests, as panellists on a programme like *Question Time* (which might also involve assessing potential questions from the studio audience) or as members of the public filmed for something like *That's Life* because they have a dog that can bark the opening bars of the Hallelujah Chorus.

In documentaries, some of these areas will overlap and a researcher will find much of the information on which the programme is based, many of the people who will be filmed or interviewed and will probably also be required to find visual material in the form of stills or archive film. Researchers tend to specialize: contestant research for quiz shows is a more highly skilled job than it might appear to the casual viewer. Someone who is a natural for *The Price is Right* will probably not be *Mastermind* material. Film research is another area where an amount of expertise is necessary but, on the whole, the average researcher will not be an expert in one area but an expert at finding experts.

Although many directors do their own research, their skills and priorities tend to be different. Film-makers are, or should be, essentially visual in their approach whereas a researcher is primarily concerned with facts. This is not to say that the average director doesn't give tuppence what is said so long as the pictures look pretty or a researcher wouldn't know a good visual image if it arrived with a sprig of holly on top. The researcher must be aware of what will come across well on screen and a director does have to be certain that what is said is accurate. But a director has other responsibilities, like budgeting, logistics, editing, and so on while, inevitably, research takes its place as only one of a number of factors. A researcher can, however, concentrate on the one task and should be able to do that in greater depth.

The researcher should keep in mind the visual potential of the material. Instead of having a clip of an expert talking, cutaway to a still of something mentioned, back to the talking head, cutaway to library footage, talking head, noddy shot of interviewers and talking head again, consider other possibilities. Would a dramatic reconstruction put across a point better? Try, however, to employ real actors. I, and I bet most viewers, cringe with embarrassment when ordinary members of the public are filmed re-enacting an event. You've seen someone walk into a suburban living-room, apparently oblivious of an entire film crew huddled in one corner, and say, 'I'm from The Adoption Society' in painfully enunciated tones.

Beware, however, of what's called the Lord Privy Seal syndrome. An early David Frost sketch satirized the tendency of news programmes to overdo illustrative stills. As a fake item about the government was read, there appeared on screen in quick succession a photograph of an ermine-clad figure (Lord), a lavatory (Privy) and finally a performing animal (seal).

Essential Qualities

Just gathering material is not enough; it needs to be interpreted and assessed. Governments are notoriously prone to change methods of calculation when they don't like the statistics on trade, inflation, unemployment or whatever, so instead of uncritically reproducing the latest PR handout from the Ministry of Truth, a good researcher would look at the criteria used in calculating the figures. If they have been changed since the last time, it might be of interest to get them recalculated using the original criteria and see what emerges.

A researcher also needs initiative. A producer may ask for certain facts but good research does not consist of collecting them and them only. Supplementary information or additional material which leads on from what was requested is useful and, even if it doesn't change the direction of the programme from the original plan, it might form the basis of another item.

In an ideal world, there would be time for every item to be researched thoroughly but something like a daily news programme considers, perforce, in-depth background research a luxury. The story may not be written before the research is done, but the outline will already have been drawn and it is simply the researcher's job to fill it in. In cases like this it's often more a question of what's available rather than what's best. Television is a visual medium so items may be done only if there are stills or film clips to illustrate a story.

Even if film is available, it may not be possible to obtain it in time or, if it is coming from an outside source, it may be too expensive. The same applies to interviewees; the producer of a chat show might want the latest Oscar-winning actor but half-an-hour before transmission, if the said actor is stuck in a traffic jam fifty miles away or his agent is demanding too high a fee, might accept the humblest RSC spear-carrier who happens to be appearing in a Schools Drama in the studio next door. So the researcher must be aware of timescales and the number of alternatives that can feasibly be tried within that time.

On a multi-part documentary there is more time to try for the ideal rather than settling for the available and to explore fascinating by-ways. This inevitably means that a greater proportion of the work done will not find its way to the screen. All the same, filming and transmission dates will impose limits, so the researcher will again have to be prepared to make judgements about which aspects of the work need the most time spent on them. You can take a whole year to find one three-minute clip of film that all the experts agree was lost. This is certainly a coup, but if you did nothing else in that time, what is going to fill the other ten thousand, seven hundred and ninety-seven minutes of the proposed series?

Getting Ideas

A lot of programmes, particularly the magazine format ones, rely on researchers to come up with ideas for items.

Developing contacts to get stories first in an area, be it the fashion industry, farming, medicine, the City or whatever is vital. So is reading the specialist press and noting any future events that might form the basis of a film or studio piece. Keep a diary of future stories that might be worth covering, so that when the production team is looking for something to cover in next week's programme you can astound everyone round the table with your knowledge of what is going on, based on items gathered weeks or months previously.

The ability to find an unusual angle on the most banal and obvious story is something that can't really be taught, but is what distinguishes a good researcher from an indispensable one. Often this is just a matter of knowing what will appeal to the producer or editor of your show.

You also need to be able to fight for your ideas. It's not up to the researcher to say whether an item or programme should or should not be done, but you need to marshal your evidence and present your views succinctly. There's nothing worse than going to your grave convinced that an idea that was rejected would have changed the face of the documentary as we know it. And if you plough miserably on when you are convinced a project is doomed to failure, you will not only have a very unhappy time, you will also get your share of the blame when the programme falls flat on its face.

Learn your boss's buzz words; having an idea is one thing, selling it another. Saying 'This is a really *relevant* story', when the current word is 'crucial' may mean that your idea is seen as yesterday's news. You can use the converse to damn a story. 'I think it was relevant a few months ago, but things have moved on a bit since then, it's not really crucial now' is guaranteed to give any producer pause for thought.

So far the picture that emerges of the ideal researcher is an appealing one; enthusiastic, persistent, hard-working, able to think laterally, to come up with an inexhaustible supply of original ideas and present them in a way irresistible to the hardened cynicism of an editor who's seen it all before. There's one other essential attribute, the ability to carry cans. When a programme is successful, the producer and/or director will preen themselves, modestly accept compliments and may even go up to collect an award. If it is a failure, the cry might well go up ... 'the research wasn't very good'.

This is not the place to discuss how to deal with office politics, how to ensure that you're not made the scapegoat for others' incompetence and all the other elements of working life. There are any number of books on the subject: this one just aims to give an introduction to the practical skills of television research.

Chapter 2

Finding Facts

I started collecting material on AIDS while working for *Newsnight* in the early Eighties because it seemed as if it could turn out to be an important story. On the other hand, it might be a passing problem, soon solved. At that time AIDS seemed to be confined to a very small proportion of Americans, thousands of miles away and therefore of only minor interest to the Great British Public. In only a few years it has, of course, become a major issue with articles in the media almost daily, international seminars, a controversial government advertising campaign and something of which everyone, from school children to pensioners, has heard.

When I first started collecting information, the only material available came from American sources and what were then thought of as 'the facts' seem in retrospect to be laughably off-target. The first reports suggested that the development of the syndrome was linked to the use of sodium amytal poppers by some sections of the gay community. Another theory was that the disease might be connected to feline leukaemia since cases of AIDS and cases of cats with a form of leukaemia appeared in the same area.

I tell you this, not to impress with my prescience and eye for a good story, but to point out that facts are not the solid certainties the word suggests. Both those theories about the cause of AIDS looked, at the time they were published, to be based on sound scientific reasoning. Even now, new strains of the disease are being found, new theories about its nature developed and new methods of treatment devised. Some will have greater validity than others, but many questions have no definitive answers yet.

When working on current affairs issues there are basically two forms of factual research. The first consists of collecting what is generally agreed to be the facts of the case and the second, the exposé method, is to collect facts that have either not been considered or which have been rejected by the general consensus. Facts by themselves are merely a list of statements — what makes a programme is the interpretation of them. A glass is half full or half empty. There is no dispute about the amount of liquid in it, only how the complete picture is perceived.

Sources

Your job as a researcher for current affairs consists mainly of finding experts to offer their opinions and tell you on what they base them. Sources, even in this computer age, are still largely found in printed form; newspapers, periodicals or books. If you are working in current affairs, access to a good cuttings library is essential. Every daily or weekly programme relies heavily on print journalism. Keeping up with the specialist press in your area is also a good idea. *Willings Press Guide* contains details.

Government departments are an excellent source of statistics. They should always be approached through the press office of the department concerned. However, all statistics and opinion polls need to be treated with a degree of caution. I once read and analysed some seven hundred letters about holidays received from members of the public who had been invited to write in with their experiences. Not unnaturally, most of them had complaints — well, would you go to all the trouble of writing to say nothing had gone wrong and you'd had a lovely time? There seemed to be a large number of correspondents who had received a raw deal from one company in particular, but further research showed this was the one that handled most package holidays in this country. Obviously there would be a greater proportion about it because of the size of their share of the market. The whole exercise seemed to me fairly futile; the sample was self-selected, there was no attempt to match holidays for cost, location or anything else and one particularly lurid account the director followed up turned out to be a pack of lies. We had no way of checking the accuracy of all seven hundred accounts.

You should, of course, treat the conclusions drawn from facts with some scepticism, but you will have to make a decision or you'll have no programme. If you have the time, explore as many sources as possible — not just the easiest to find and actively look for differing conclusions or for differing sets of facts from less obvious sources.

Contemporary Research

I'm always amazed and pleased at the willingness of experts to do my work for me. In 1980 I was working for *Out of Court*, a weekly magazine programme about the law. Parliament had just debated whether to abolish Section 4 of the 1824 Vagrancy Act, commonly known as 'sus', i.e. suspicion that a crime might have been about to be committed.

I was asked to find out about 'sus' laws in other countries. The French and American embassies put me in touch with their own lawyers in London whom I rang on the Friday. They were both very interested and gulped only slightly when I said I needed the information for Monday afternoon or Tuesday morning at the latest. They both slaved away over the weekend to give me details of their respective countries' statutes and, in the case of the French, a potted history of the introduction and abolition of a sus law during and immediately after the French Revolution. American states all have different statutes and their lawyer gave me a detailed tour of all fifty-two plus a recent Supreme Court decision. I also rang a journal devoted to Commonwealth law and the editor turned up an interesting case in New Zealand. Lest you think it was all too easy, I should add that the German embassy's lawyer simply said, 'In our country we have no such law' and put the 'phone down on me.

In television, we blithely assume that people will drop everything to help and that they are so often willing to do so is a source of great relief. In return, I think the least you as the researcher can do is cheer them up a bit. Gentle flattery never comes amiss — how many people can bring themselves to be rude and turn you down if you say humbly 'I'm told you're an expert on.....?' After all, they aren't to know that you might be using the very same words to the next person on your list. And if you engage their attention by finding an aspect of their work that is a little out of the ordinary, as I did for the *Out of Court* research, it will pay dividends. The American lawyer was particularly enthusiastic because, as emerged in the general chat that preceded my asking him the main questions, I found he was an anglophile and an enthusiast for the history of law. By suggesting that surely much American law was based on English but how about places like Texas that had once been Spanish? I was able to persuade him to do much of my research for me. When he rang back after the weekend, he read me great chunks of the New York statutes which were, in their wording, very similar to laws passed in England in the sixteenth century against rogues and vagabonds. This was only of passing interest to my programme, but I listened patiently and was suitably and genuinely grateful for all the work he had put in.

Historical Research

Trying to ascertain the facts of a current situation or something within living memory is difficult enough but at least you can go back and ask supplementary questions if there's something you don't understand or what appears to be a gap in the facts. Historical research is very different. Say you're doing a programme on that perennial question 'Who killed the Princes in the Tower?' You would only be doing this if someone has come up with a startling new theory or if you are expected to find a new candidate yourself.

In cases like this, you would start by reading the many books published about the murder (or even deaths: both lads might have died of natural causes); you can talk to historians and Ph.D. researchers working on the period but each will allocate a different degree of importance to the known facts. What you will now have to do is add original material from primary sources, but where do you start? First, look at the bibliographies in the serious books on the subject (anything without a bibliography is not serious). This will list other books and magazine articles on the subject and refer to primary sources, i.e. contemporary documents. These latter may also be quoted in the text, but only the sections supporting the writer's theory will appear so you'll probably have to re-read them yourself.

From the bibliographies you will be able to see what has not been considered. For example, has anyone used the foreign state papers for the period? Diplomats were then, as now, largely engaged in an intelligence operation for their own government back home and there may be reports sent to the French or Dutch monarchs which may provide interesting clues.

The Vatican library should also be considered; the Roman Catholic Church, after all, was then the major force in Europe. Did any of these foreign ambassadors leave private papers which have found their way into a national archive or are they still in their descendants' possession?

For this type of research what you are not told is usually of more interest than what you are. Read biographies of contemporaries; a casual reference to a journey that was made unexpectedly might give you pause for thought. And if a major figure was not present at an important meeting or occasion, is there a reason for his absence that might provide other clues to be followed up?

With a great deal of factual research you will mainly be working with negatives, filling gaps and you will have to accept that there may never be a final answer, short of discovering an ancient bit of parchment that says 'I killed ye Princes in ye Tower, signed Richard ye Third'. In this case, you would know it was a fake because numbering kings I, II, III, etc. began after Richard's reign, and anyway he'd have signed himself in Latin.

Always be alert to the possibility of forgery in documents, and always ask yourself 'What is this person's interest?' Sir Thomas More wrote a biography of Richard III, putting the blame for the murders squarely on him, and this work, heavily spiced as it is with gossipy, apparently first-hand detail, has influenced writers from Shakespeare to Sir Winston Churchill. Yet More was only seven years old when the king died. An alert researcher would discover that More was employed by the son of Richard's usurper. This doesn't mean that all the facts in the book are wrong, merely that they've been well and truly interpreted. You may not be a specialist in the area of fifteenth century history so in the course of the research you will need to consult someone who is an expert in the field with whom to check your findings.

Using an Expert

Most documentary series on historical subjects use an expert to advise them. The reason they don't use the experts themselves to do the research is because academics and television researchers work from different starting points. To over-simplify, academics work largely from written sources while programmes are primarily about visual images or, in the case of more recent history, people talking about their experiences. An expert is therefore employed to advise on likely areas of interest and as a fact checker. If you are interviewing a member of the public about events that took place in even the comparatively recent past, they may well unintentionally mislead you. For example, can you say off the top of your head when decimalisation came in? Or the date of the introduction of colour television? Someone being filmed for their memories of an event may well get the date wrong and your expert should pick that up.

A bit of advice about using experts; they are being paid for their expertise so if they suggest reading a particular book, do read it. And if you want them to answer a particular question, allow enough time for the necessary research to be completed. It's no use ringing up from the dubbing theatre to ask when an obscure Act of Parliament was passed and expect an immediate answer.

Libraries and Record Offices

You will find that much factual research is done in libraries, which will often have different classification systems. Finding your way round catalogues is an art; make friends with the librarian. Libraries are increasingly cost-conscious and ordering books through your local branch library can be expensive. You may be better off getting a reader's ticket for a specialist library and doing two or three weeks intensive work there.

Before you go to a library you haven't used before, do ring up and check the opening hours, whether you need a ticket and what the regulations are for getting one. Do you, for example, require a letter from someone in authority in your organisation? A telephone call will also save you a lot of time if you discover that the information you want isn't there. This may sound blindingly obvious but in a large city the papers you want to study might be in the local County Record Office, the University Library (because the original owners deposited them there) or the diocesan library if the subject has something to do with the Church.

The Church played a large, non-spiritual, as well as spiritual, part in the lives of most people before the nineteenth century. It was long a major landowner and remains today the landlord of a considerable amount of property. Church courts held jurisdiction over matters such as probate and moral issues like adultery, which now is considered a question of personal conscience. Parish councils fulfilled many of the functions, such as welfare benefits, now handled by local or central government. The Church's role in education has always been fundamental.

Other large organisations, such as political parties, commercial companies, friendly societies, etc., also have records which may still be in their own hands. Some have an official archivist or historian, others may be able to put you in touch with an unofficial historian, usually an ex-member of staff, who has an interest in the subject.

A Note on Dates

When working with historical documents, there are several factors about dating which need to be taken into consideration. Very early English documents used a variety of calendars, including the Roman calendar (beware the Ides of March!), often on the whim of the writer. By the end of the twelfth century, 25th March was generally taken to be New Year's Day, i.e. a document dated 24th March 1650 would actually be 1651 by our reckoning. Parts of the Continent from 1582 and Scotland from 1600 started to consider 1st January as New Year's Day. This can explain many apparent anomalies in correspondence between England and other countries.

This is by no means the least of the researcher's worries. Until 1582 the Julian calendar was used in all Christian countries. By that time the tropical and calendar years had become seriously out of step, so Pope Gregory ordered that 5th October should become 15th October and the timing of leap years should also be altered. The new calendar was gradually adopted throughout the Christian world and in 1752 Great Britain finally caught up. By an act passed in 1751, the day following 31st December 1751 became 1st January 1752 and 3rd September 1752 became 14th September. Since that time, Britain and Europe and their colonies have all agreed on the date.

Between 1582 and 1752 you need to find out which calendar was being used in which country if you are dealing with England's relations with anywhere overseas, or even over Hadrian's wall. The Muslim, Jewish, Chinese and Japanese still have calendars which are reckoned on different bases from the Christian calendar.

Pre-Reformation documents were often dated according to the liturgical calendar, e.g. 24th August would appear as St Bartholomew's Day. *The Oxford Companion to English Literature* lists saints' days and church feasts and shows you how to calculate the date of Easter for any year. It also gives regnal years, used to date Acts of Parliament and some legal documents.

Overseas Sources

Most of the facts about foreign countries that you are likely to need in day-to-day programme-making can be obtained in this country. Statistics are available from the embassies, from the Foreign & Commonwealth Office, the Department of Trade & Industry or from the British offices of international organisations such as the United Nations or the European Community.

Only if you are doing historical research will you need to use record offices and libraries overseas. Speaking the relevant language is only a very small part of the work; you need to be able to find your way around the records first. Although, broadly speaking, most countries have equivalents to the British Public Record Office, county or local authority records and ecclesiastical records, material may not be distributed between them in the same way as it is here.

The law, especially relating to property and inheritance, will certainly be different. You have not got time to learn about the legal history of another country so, although it may seem expensive, hire an expert, an academic who has experience in the country and the period you are working on.

Chapter 3

Finding People

This falls into three categories: 1. looking for a specific person whose name or at least identity is known; 2. looking for someone whose experience is representative of a group of people, such as the homeless; 3. looking for someone to put across a point of view, an expert or a spokesperson. Celebrity and contestant research falls into categories one and two respectively.

Specific People

My first major research job for the BBC was to track down a group of people who had, eighteen years previously, appeared on *Panorama* doing their school nativity play. At that time they were at a primary school in North London and in different classes, so their ages, when I was looking for them, would have been between twenty-two and twenty-nine. Altogether some fifty children appeared in the film clip, of whom thirty-odd played major roles, the rest being the heavenly choir.

In the end, I found all but three of the 'stars' of the show. Since two were brother and sister, I count that as failing to locate only two and half, but even now it rankles that I didn't get them all. In odd moments, I wonder what else I could have done to make my record 100%.

I started off by getting photographs made from various frames of the film clip, showing as many of the children as possible in as big a close-up as possible. With the photographs, I went to the school where, luckily, two of the teachers involved in the original production still worked. With the aid of old registers and the help of the music teacher (now retired) who had coached the choir, about twenty of the children were identified and their old addresses noted.

For most people, the twenties are the time of most mobility and change, both in jobs and accommodation, so I concentrated on finding their parents. This had an additional bonus; they remembered, better than their children, that period of their lives and were more helpful with clues about what had happened to the families who had moved out of the area.

Some parents still lived at their old address, which I checked with the telephone directory and the electoral register (of which more below). I wrote to the parents on BBC headed paper. Except where time is at a premium, I think writing is important. It establishes your credentials and should reassure the recipient that you're not a hoaxer or a private detective about to rattle skeletons in closets.

Next, taking the photographs, I interviewed the children I had found so far. Where possible, the parents came along too but I spoke to each person separately before chatting to the whole group. I didn't want the children to be inhibited about recalling things they still didn't want their parents to know, but the group conversation (which often included brothers and sisters and even neighbours whose children, though not in the play, had also attended the school) was important to spark off memories on both sides.

These interviews put more names to faces and gave me useful clues to follow up about those who had moved out of the area. 'I think they went to Northampton, or was it Nottingham?', 'Didn't he go into the Army?', 'I still see her mother round here from time to time'.

This last remark sent me off to the local library to go through electoral registers, which are a very useful tool. Not everyone appears in the telephone directory; some people are ex-directory, some live in rented accommodation where there may be a pay-'phone or one in the landlord's name and even today there are a surprising number of people who don't have a telephone. Directory Enquiries will tell you if the number is ex-directory, in which case you can write, and at least you've got confirmation that the person you need is at that address. But what you often find useful are electoral registers.

With more precise information, 'He lives in that big block of flats at the end of the High Street', you can find an address over the 'phone. I've always found library staff very willing to help with this kind of query, although some local authorities do ban such information being given by telephone. However, electoral registers must be on the open shelves so a trip to the library may be necessary. Alternatively, neighbouring authorities may have a copy and the British Library has a complete set.

Electoral registers may be useful in looking for someone who has moved. The current inhabitant of the flat or house (with the name, you can get the telephone number) may have an address to forward mail or remember whereabouts the person you are seeking now lives. Even something as imprecise as 'He went to Oxfordshire, a village with a funny name' narrows your search.

Searching electoral registers is not the high spot of any researcher's life but if it needs to be done, it needs to be done thoroughly. A ruler run down the page stops your eye skipping — you can bet the one time you do glance swiftly over a page, expecting the name to leap out, it will be lurking modestly at the bottom of the sheet and you'll miss it. I took with me a list of all the as-yet-unlocated children in case they or their families were still in the same area. There is, however, no point in noting and writing to every Smith, Jones and Brown. The same applies to telephone directories. It is worth ringing through fifty people with the right name if you're really desperate, but any more than that and I think you're wasting time that might be better employed trying some other route.

I found some of the children I still needed through the registers but quite a few remained untraced. The next step was to get a bit of publicity for the search. An advertisement in a newspaper will help, particularly if you are looking for a specific group of people, such as left-handed divorcees with twins. Even better, however, is to get an article written about what you are doing.

In this case, both the local paper and the *Daily Mirror* ran the story of the search and carried a photograph of one of the children we were particularly anxious to trace as she appeared in an important sequence in the original film. A woman rang to say it was her daughter and I duly set up an interview. It was not the person I was looking for; there had been two girls with the same name in the school. I never did work out whether the woman genuinely did not recognise her own daughter.... You do need to be quite cautious with members of the public; a surprising number will say what they think you want to hear in order to appear on screen.

Another of the major stars of the show was particularly difficult to find. A clue that she had been a very clever child had me ringing round universities to find out if she had been a student; this would have yielded the result in the end because she had done a Ph.D. thesis but, in fact, the *Daily Mirror* article led her to ring us about six weeks after it appeared. She hadn't read the article, but the ripples caused by it had finally spread via ex-neighbours, friends and family to the groves of academe. I was pleased at the demonstration of the power of the press; I had no idea there were so many universities, colleges, polytechnics, teacher training colleges and art schools in the UK. And, of course, despite her cleverness she might never have gone on to further education.

She might also have married before taking her degree, especially if she had been a mature student. One of the major problems involved in tracing women is that most change their names on marriage. The place to find out whether anyone you are looking for has married, and after all most people do, is St Catherine's House for England and Wales, Register House in Edinburgh for Scotland and in Northern Ireland the General Register Office. The Isle of Man and the Channel Islands also have separate registers. As well as indices to births, marriages and deaths since 1837, St Catherine's House also has records of divorces, adoptions and some certificates relating to events which took place abroad or at sea.

Generally, if you're trying to track someone down, go for the most recent event. Someone who married ten years ago (and you would find this information in the marriage index) probably has children and it is their birth certificates that will give the most up-to-date information. The indices give only the briefest details; names of those marrying, the area in which they married or the name of the child, the mother's maiden name and, again, the area in which the birth was registered. To get home addresses, names of witnesses or any further detail you will have to order a certificate. The procedure is explained there.

One lad had gone into the Church. He was simple to find: I just looked him up in *Crockford's Clerical Directory*, the Who's Who of the Anglican church, which lists all clergy and their livings throughout the world. All the other major denominations have similar publications. Most professions, such as the law or medicine, also have directories.

Trade associations, like the Institute of Sprocket Manufacturers or whatever, can also be useful and it's worth trying relevant unions if you know, for example, that the person you are looking for is a boiler-maker. However, not everyone belongs to either a trade association or union.

If you do track someone down via the company they work for or an association to which they belong, the organisation may not be willing to give out an address or telephone number without checking with the person concerned that they are willing to talk to you. In cases like this, they should be prepared either to telephone the individual and give your telephone number or to pass on a letter written by you and sent c/o the organisation.

Although this wasn't a method I used on this particular programme, you may have some luck via mailing lists. Everyone, but everyone, gets junk mail and, if you know that the person you are looking for is a social worker but doesn't belong either to the professional body or the trade union, it might be worth finding out if (s)he's on a mailing list or subscribes to a trade journal.

In all, I had six months to find thirty-odd people for the programme. At the beginning, it seemed like a very long time but there were stretches within that period when every avenue turned out to be a blind alley. On other days, three 'phone calls might locate three more children. For this kind of programme you need stamina and persistence.

The ability to think laterally is essential. Every scrap of information about a person provides a clue to be followed up. Hobbies may mean membership of a club or association or even a way of making a living. Don't limit yourself to one person only — other members of the family should be able to put you in touch, so bear in mind the possibility of finding parents, siblings or other relatives. A very rare name or a double-barrelled name in a telephone directory, even if the initials and the area are wrong, may lead you to a second-cousin or a great-aunt.

And what of the three children I didn't find? On the face of it, the brother and sister looked quite easy to trace. The family were 'known to the social services'. But a combination of official reticence 'We aren't allowed to give out that kind of information' and official incompetence 'We can tell you that they moved out of this area, but we can't find where their file was passed on to' finally led me to admit defeat. I was spending too much time on these two that I could have been devoting to the others I needed to find.

And the other boy? I never even managed to identify him with any certainty. He had only been at the school for a short while before his family moved away and, although various people thought they could put a name to the face, the trouble was they couldn't agree on the name.

Representatives and Spokespersons

Finding people in general is easier in some ways and harder in others. If you are looking for a specific person, once he or she is found, that is the end of the search. When you are looking for a representative, choices about the best have to be made. Current affairs programmes spend a lot of time looking for case histories, people whose situation typifies the effects of some law, social problem or injustice. Some present themselves by contacting a programme directly or through a pressure group. Alternatively, a producer may decide to make a film about the effects of, for example, a particular change in the law and you will be asked to find people whose story illustrates the subject.

Let's say, for the sake of example, that in this case the producer wants to do something on compensation for the victims of crime. There is a support group for people who have suffered in this way which is listed in *The Self-Help Guide*, a directory of self-help groups throughout the country. There may well be a pressure group dedicated to changes in the law which the support group will tell you about. Both organisations will be able to produce the kind of people you need for the programme.

Alternatively, you could try local law centres and Citizens' Advice Bureaux who deal with a wider variety of problems. It's worth maintaining contacts with groups who will bring cases to you if you work regularly in the current affairs field.

You have your human interest angle but you will also need a legal expert to comment on the law. The pressure group may have a tame lawyer but, if they can't suggest someone or the point at issue is a highly academic or esoteric one, the next area to explore is the specialist press. There is a journal covering every field of human work or interest and they are listed in *Willings Press Guide*, an annual directory of all newspapers and periodicals in this country and many published abroad. I have always found the journalists of the specialist press immensely knowledgeable and helpful.

As well as your legal expert, you may need a spokesperson from the government or, depending on the story, some other public body or large organisation. Most of these have someone who is used to dealing with the media. For any government department or large organisation, you must go through the press office to get statements, spokespersons or indeed any information at all, even if you do know to whom you wish to speak.

Problems arise with experts in areas that are not often in the public eye. Say a political crisis blows up on Loyalty Island. Once you've got out the atlas and discovered it's part of the New Caledonia group in the Pacific Ocean and it belongs to the French, you can start looking for your expert. It's doubtful that the French Embassy will know much about it, but they may be willing to put up a spokesperson to represent their government's views.

After many 'phone calls, it emerges that the world expert on this island is a Ph.D. student in anthropology at the University of the Outer Hebrides. While the production assistant tries to find flights that will bring the student to a studio and books lines to record an interview, you must try to find out whether he or she will come across well. In a case like this, you've got to take what you can get or not do the item. How do you find out if an interviewee is worth using?

The Interview

Experts and what might be termed ordinary people are used in programmes for three principal reasons: personal opinion, emotion or anecdote. Although your facts may also come from the people you are interviewing, information is generally better conveyed by commentary or graphics, so interviewees will be asked to give opinions, recall feelings or tell stories.

In an ideal world, we ought to meet interviewees face-to-face before inflicting them on the viewing public but, as often happens in current affairs, you may have to make an assessment of how someone will come across on screen on the basis of a telephone conversation alone.

First, make a list of questions. You don't have to stick rigidly to it, but it does help to give the conversation a framework and to serve as an *aide-memoire* to areas that have to be covered. If, however, something interesting not on your list comes up, pursue that line and then return to your list.

Over the telephone you can't see if a person has some annoying or distracting mannerism or disturbing physical characteristic, but you can find out if he or she is a reasonably fluent talker, can put over ideas clearly and concisely and recognises the rules of the game. Interviewees who start taking it personally when a questioner plays devil's advocate and puts forward alternative views or criticisms should be ruled out, largely for their own sakes as they will look silly.

It's a good idea to play less informed than you are, to appear to know nothing about a subject. That, after all, is the position of the majority of viewers and it allows you to find out if the interviewee can explain something simply. Anyone who gets tetchy about having to explain in words of less than four syllables is probably not the best choice.

If you are working on a programme that allows the luxury of meeting potential contributors before filming, you have a better chance of getting the best interviewees rather than the simply adequate. Say you are involved in a documentary series about changes in industrial processes and you want to interview ordinary people who were affected by such changes. You have collected the names and addresses of a large number of people scattered throughout the country who may have something interesting to contribute. Set up interviews in areas; go to a hotel in a large town and interview as many people as you can within that area. Write and confirm the day and time that you will be arriving.

Where possible, interview people in their own homes. They will be more relaxed and are likely to be more open with you, so you will get a better idea of what they are like. There is another advantage; they may have photographs or other useful material there which you can look at if your conversation reminds them of something relevant.

The major advantage of interviewing people face-to-face is, of course, to see them. Try to imagine the person on screen. You may have a much-loved relative with a squint that you no longer notice but, for most of your audience, it will be a distraction that will be of more interest than what is being said. Remember that pictures are the primary point of a programme and they are what the viewer concentrates on at the expense of words.

The same applies to verbal mannerisms. Anyone who says, 'Know what I mean?' every three or four words or who stammers can be ruled out, unless you are doing a programme about inarticulacy or speech defects.

Foreign and regional accents aren't too much of a problem unless it takes a while to tune in to them. I once interviewed an eminent Swedish scientist and for the first twenty minutes or so, although his use of English was grammatically impeccable, I could understand what he was saying only with difficulty. After that, as I became accustomed to his accent and rhythm of speech, I found him easy to comprehend. But the viewer will not have that amount of time.

For a big documentary you will interview many, many more people than will be filmed but, if you make it clear from the beginning that it is unlikely the interviewees will be used, they will not put themselves out to remember as much as possible or to help you. On the other hand, make no promises you can't keep. Be evasive and always write, especially if someone is filmed and then not used. Carefully phrased consolation can help soothe wounded pride.

It's up to you how to record interviews. Most researchers use a small cassette recorder but this can make interviewees self-conscious. If the person really is badly disconcerted after a short while, put the machine away, but remember that a full film crew is infinitely more off-putting.

Scribbling notes while a person talks has overtones of 'Anything you say may be taken down....' Just listening and writing up notes as soon as possible afterwards has advantages; the knowledge that there is no mechanical backup concentrates the mind wonderfully and if you can't remember anything that was said, the chances are that the interviewee was boring beyond belief.

Bear in mind that you don't need facts from your interviewees. Someone who can explain the technical workings of a revolutionary machine but who has no opinion about how it changed an industry, cannot put across his feelings about it and has no anecdotes to tell about either its invention or use, is not worth considering.

Emotion is difficult to re-create, unless it is something very disturbing. I once interviewed a woman whose face lit up in a way that surprised and delighted me when she said that after leaving school she went to work for Marks & Spencer. Further questioning elicited the fact that, as a child, going to Marks & Spencer had been a great treat for her and her mother. Her ambition had been to work there and, when she achieved it, she was not disappointed. It had been one of the happiest times of her life. But would her face light up in that magical way again for the cameras? No. It's regrettable but only really unhappy emotions can usually be evoked when the interviewee is surrounded by all the paraphenalia of a film crew.

Contestant Research

We've all sat comfortably at home, slumped in an armchair, a glass of something stimulating at hand and watched in disbelief as a hapless contestant on a quiz programme fails to come up with the name of the current Prime Minister. 'I could do better than that!' we cry scornfully. Well, yes, perhaps we can in our own homes, but could we in the alien environment of a studio, perched uncomfortably on a futuristic set with five thousand watts beating down from the lights? A surprising number of people are willing to risk making fools of themselves like this in the hope of winning a wok and finding them is the job of the contestant researcher.

About fifteen thousand people a series reckon they could do better than the average contestant on *Bob's Full House* but they can't all be interviewed and tested. Most television companies have a standard application form for each quiz programme they do and hopeful contestants are asked to fill one in, giving details of age, occupation, hobbies and interests, etc., which has to be returned with a photograph.

It cannot be emphasised enough that television is primarily a visual medium and the people who appear on quiz shows have to be not stunningly good looking but at least of an animated and cheerful appearance. They have to have, as one contestant researcher told me, 'a television face'. She couldn't really define this, but she knows it when she sees it.

Specialist quizzes, like *Mastermind* or *Film Buff of the Year*, obviously have different criteria but this section mainly deals with the more general kind of quiz programme.

After the first weeding of those who look terminally depressed or whose application forms reveal a degree of illiteracy incompatible with the level of knowledge required by the show, the next stage is to interview all those who look as if they have potential. This will probably be about two thousand people and it's easier to interview in regions round the country than to get everyone to come to your town or city, especially as very few companies have the resources to pay the travelling costs of everyone they interview.

As well as those who write in individually, you will probably get a good response from social clubs and the regional offices of large companies, like chain stores. They can be found in *The Directory of British Associations* or local telephone directories. You are looking for confident, outgoing people who want to enjoy themselves and such people are usually members of social organisations or work in a field that involves a lot of contact with others, like the police or the armed forces.

Stay in a hotel in a reasonably central town or city with good transport facilities so that people living in small villages can travel easily. Book another room in which to conduct the interviews. It's probably superfluous to say at this stage that if you want to work in this very specialised area of research you must enjoy meeting people and you need the kind of temperament that will cope with being cheerful, encouraging and sociable for hours and days on end. You will be spending a lot of time on the road, so you can say goodbye to a private life for a couple of months at a time.

Interview people in small groups so you can see how well they react to others and how well they take to competition. A round of general knowledge questions asked individually will test their intellectual abilities and then a section where the potential contestants compete to answer first. This will both gauge their speed of reaction and show any tendency to sulk if they lose or display other unattractive qualities if they win. You will probably find that some people are too clever for your particular show; they can either be shortlisted for another quiz programme produced by your company or rejected outright. You are not looking for the winner of the quiz, that will be decided on the programme itself. What you're doing at this stage is to select people who you think have an equal chance of winning. The viewers will lose interest very early if it becomes obvious that one person is going to walk all over the opposition. Include in your questions a few which you don't expect people to be able to answer so you can weed out those who should be encouraged to try for *Mastermind* or something more intellectually challenging.

You also need to chat to the interviewees about themselves. This will give you an idea of how they will come across. Those who are shy or who don't like talking about themselves will almost certainly freeze up completely when they get to the studio, but those who are boastful or can't be shut up will alienate the viewer — and the presenter probably won't take too well to having the limelight stolen. You are looking for people who simply want to enjoy themselves. No one goes in for a quiz show in the hope of winning wealth beyond the dreams of avarice, but a very large number simply want their friends to see them on the telly or to meet celebrities. These can be ruled out.

Write notes about each potential contestant's personality, abilities and speed on the application form. There will be thousands of pieces of paper in the office and there's no point in adding to them. At this juncture, those who will be your contestants will emerge. Researchers say that an indefinable 'something' just tips the balance and the ability to recognize it is a combination of instinct and experience.

After your marathon stint interviewing round the country you will wind up with a file full of people who are suitable for your particular show. They then have to be sorted to appear on individual programmes and should be balanced according to sex, age, general knowledge and the region they come from. Try to get a good mix, but remember that older people tend to be slower, so putting an old age pensioner on a show with a number of much younger people is a mistake, even if all other factors are equal, simply because the older person will get beaten to the buzzer every time.

As well as the contestants who appear, you will need a few on standby in case someone is taken ill or after the rehearsal has a nervous breakdown and refuses to go on. It's useful to have, in addition, a number of possible contestants who live near the place where the programme is to be recorded so, in the event of a rail strike or freak weather conditions that cause chaos on the roads, you can get them into the studio quickly. If all else fails, you will have to rely on your friends.

Before the recording, you should prepare a biography of each contestant which includes anecdotes they can tell on the show or which can be used to display the quizmaster's rapier-like wit. This is given to the scriptwriters well in advance so they can prepare the ad libs.

Contestants usually arrive early on the day of recording and stay overnight. Their travel and accommodation arrangements will probably be your responsibility. Most quiz shows are recorded in blocks with at least two being done on the same day, even though they may be shown weekly. If the winner from one programme goes on to the next, ask all the contestants to bring at least one change of outfit so whoever apparently goes on to appear next week wears a different set of clothes.

Certain colours and patterns show up badly on screen so contestants have to be told not to wear black, white or cream, which are very hard to light, or red which tends to bleed. Thin stripes, small checks and busy patterns also cause problems with strobing. You can either ask your people to bring a choice of outfits which can be tested in front of the cameras or make sure that the wardrobe department has a few dresses or shirts in reserve.

Having got them all safely to the studio, you will spend most of your time keeping the contestants calm but entertained while hanging around for their big moment. It is only at this point that it hits some people just what they have let themselves in for and you will probably find yourself soothing and reassuring at least one person who's beginning to think again about the whole caper. A degree in psychology comes in handy.

Celebrity Research

Chat shows need celebrities and celebrities need chat shows: in biology this is called symbiosis, two forms of life which co-exist to the benefit of both. Viewers like to see famous people chatting about their life and times and the famous people like to appear because the viewers, who go to see their films or buy their books, make them famous and rich.

Usually people appear on chat shows because they have something they want to plug, but some people are such mega-stars that they can, especially if they never give television interviews, be welcomed whenever they want to appear. A regular letter to the star's manager or agent saying that the programme is still interested in interviewing the star at any time should be sent out, but you won't usually get a positive response until the said mega-star has something to sell.

Managers and agents are the really powerful people in show biz, so people who go into celebrity research tend to have a background which has given them a lot of contacts in the industry. These contacts will keep you informed about what is going on and also help when it comes to approaching an agent, because one of his or her clients is doing something of interest.

Usually, however, the agent will get in touch with you to say that a client is publishing an autobiography or designing a new range of jewellery for cats and would you like the person on your programme?

In the early days of the chat show, it often seemed that whichever channel you turned on, there was the same celebrity, telling the same stories — the only thing that varied was the presenter asking the questions. Now the major chat shows (as I write, *Wogan*, *Aspel & Company* and Clive James' various programmes) do not interview someone who has recently appeared or is due to appear on one of the other programmes.

This may conjure up a picture of desperate competition with dark deeds of skulduggery to prevent the other side getting to a celebrity first, but the reality is less exciting. Chat shows all have a precisely defined audience and are rarely in the market for the same people. As the researcher, you must know who your audience is and what they want. You may be knocked out by an avant-garde poet who has just brought out a slim volume of verse castigating every aspect of British society. If, however, your audience consists of people who have just come in from a hard day at work and want something cheerful to slump in front of, the last thing they need is an intellectually demanding moan.

It is also essential to get a good mix of people on the show to pull in as many different components of your potential audience as possible. Three film actors, three writers or three footballers all on the same show will mean that you lose the members of your audience who don't go to the cinema, who never read a book or who hate sport. One of each will attract the readers who hate sport, the cinema-goers who don't read, etc. You will also run into problems with the agents who will all demand top billing and the most time for their particular client.

Chat show hosts are usually around only for the recording or, if it goes out live, the transmission of their programmes. This means that the major responsibility falls to the producer and the researchers, although the host will, depending on temperament, contribute to a greater or lesser extent to the choice of guests.

Each guest who appears will be seen and talked with by a researcher. Quite often you will find yourself trying to assess someone who has very little television experience or indeed who has never appeared on screen. You may be confronted by a reclusive accountant who has just written a bestseller and the same criteria will apply here as in other areas of television where ordinary members of the public appear. But, and this is a big but, on a chat show your reclusive accountant will have to be able to hold the audience's attention simply by what (s)he says for a relatively long period of time. If the interviewee is paralysed by fright or runs out of steam after two minutes with another eight to fill, there is nowhere to cut to but the interviewer whose role, after all, is to get the guest to talk. If your show is live, without any possibility of editing out long, embarrassing silences, the problems are quadrupled.

It is therefore essential to try and get a copy of something on which the guest has already appeared, even if it's only a three-minute spot on a regional news magazine programme. A radio interview can also give you an idea of what (s)he is like, but remember that radio interviews are edited. You might, based on your conversation, decide that the interviewee is worth risking if (s)he is very outgoing and confident with a lot to say but do bear in mind that studios can be very daunting to those who have never encountered them before.

You might realize, within a couple of minutes, that your reclusive, bestselling accountant cannot string two sentences together without being overcome by shyness. Most people have a realistic idea of their limitations and should recognize for themselves whether or not they are right for a chat show, but for those who don't, the non-committal, evasive letter is a must.

With more experienced guests, the preliminary chat is to explore the areas that can be discussed on the show. Before you go along to talk to the celebrity, do as much research as you can. It's only sensible to read the autobiography first, especially if that's what's being plugged, or to see, if possible, the film in which your star is appearing. General background material can be obtained either from the agent or from press cuttings if no biography exists.

This is where things can get very tricky. We all have something in our past that we wouldn't like broadcast to ten million people and celebrities are just like you and me in this respect. The fact that many of the more distressing episodes of their lives have already been splashed over the tabloids does not mean they will want to talk about them. Your conversation will include not only the areas that will be covered in the show, but also the ones that in no circumstances will be mentioned. In some cases, people want to appear in order to refute stories that have been published about them which will make your job easier.

A much-married person may be willing to discuss spouses one, three and five but will not allow any references to numbers two and four. A twenty-stone comic may be happy to talk about his weight but not his baldness, even though both may be his trademarks. The host of the show needs to know which areas are taboo to prevent inadvertent reference to things that will upset the guest. The audience may find an uncomfortable refusal to discuss a topic deeply fascinating, but the host will not take kindly to being made to look a fool and the guest's agent, who probably represents many other famous people, will be very wary of dealing with you again.

If your programme has managed to offend an agent, you will find it very difficult indeed to get any of his or her clients to appear on the show. Letters written or 'phone calls made to the star will be taken by other people, or the star will pass all requests on to the agent. If you do manage to bypass the agent and the celebrity agrees to appear on the show, you may simply make matters worse: no one likes decisions arranged behind their back.

Research notes have to be very detailed so that the host will feel confident that anything the guest mentions will not come as a disconcerting surprise. If you forget to put in that the celebrity has undergone a long period of psychotherapy, the host will be badly adrift if the talk turns to 'my analyst', 'my Oedipus complex' or, in the case of ageing hippies, 'bad karma'.

First of all, the host needs to know why the guest is being wheeled on, so you start off with edited highlights of the person's career plus, of course, what is being plugged.

Then you need to give a more detailed biographical account. Ideally this should be taken from a source approved by the guest, either an autobiography or a biography made with full co-operation. Where none exists, the agent and press cuttings should be able to help. A note of caution here; for whatever reason your celebrity may want to suppress something that (s)he was once perfectly willing to divulge to the press, like exact age, children with whom all contact has since been broken or, in the case of a writer, early work of which (s)he is now ashamed. If the guest doesn't want people to know, that should be fine by you. You are not conducting a trial by television or making an alternative *This is Your Life*.

After the detailed biography, there should be a list of areas of interest which will be talked about on the show covering what you and your guest have already discussed. Note here any anecdotes that can be told. If you have any film clips to show, put them in at the appropriate place. Getting film clips may also be your job (see Chapter 4).

Naturally, the exact form the notes you give the presenter of your show will vary according to the way (s)he works. Most chat show hosts write their own scripts or may do them with the producer: like all television programmes you need to fit in with the way the team works.

Chapter 4

Finding Visual Material

FINDING VISUAL MATERIAL

Stills and Archive Film

The television researcher's work in the area of stills is made much easier by the existence of an invaluable reference book. *The Picture Researcher's Handbook* (3rd edition) lists picture libraries all over the world and their holdings. In many ways, the second edition of the book is more helpful as it contains useful information about types of pictures, e.g. woodcuts, lithographs, photographs, etc., and their history. There is also a section on the vexed and nightmarish question of copyright, which I have no intention of tackling here. There is also a section on this in another excellent book, *The Researcher's Guide to British Film and Television Collections*, but the new copyright act will modify some of the information given there. This book lists sources in Britain with details of their holdings of archive film and also has useful articles on film research and formats.

Neither is, of course, exhaustive. Depending on the kind of material you want, there are other possibilities for the researcher. If you are working on an aspect of local history, public libraries usually have a history collection which will include photographs of the area and books with illustrations that can be used as well as information about societies interested in the subject. Some areas have specific projects which aim to collect old photographs and identify the places and people in them.

Advertisements or articles in the local paper might produce someone with amateur film of the area and local film clubs may know of enthusiasts with private film collections. The local paper method, although usually effective, may not in certain instances be as useful as you might expect. People move away from areas, especially large towns or cities, as they grow older and/or more prosperous. If you are seeking material on Whitechapel fifty years ago, advertising in the *Whitechapel Gazette* may not produce many people who still live there. The Jewish population tended to move west from Whitechapel to Golders Green to Mill Hill, while the Cockneys moved east via post-war council estates to places like Romford or Harlow in

Essex. Advertising in the local papers in those areas will produce better results. People from Northern cities often retire to the coast, so find out the favoured towns and start looking there.

Commercial Feature Films

Commercial feature films are more of a problem. Film companies will usually only release certain clips of their current and recent productions and you have to take what they offer, which is not necessarily what you want. If you are doing the biography of a film actor or director, you will run into the problem of copyright ownership. *Halliwell's Film Guide* gives the name of the company that made the film, but if it is no longer in existence, it will take more research to discover who now owns the rights to the film you want to use. The British Film Institute should be able to help.

Often the rights are owned not by the film company, but by a distributor. Different distributors may own rights to the same film in different countries, which raises problems with overseas sales.

In addition to the rights owned by companies or distributors, there are other fees to be taken into account. Directors, writers, musicians, actors and even stunt performers are all entitled to residual payments. So, as a researcher, be prepared for hefty charges for feature film clips before getting too excited about a sequence.

If your budget is, however, in the big money league and your producer decides that a clip from an American movie is essential, you can save a few pence on 'phone bills by negotiating through the London office of the company. Most of the major companies have one. If the film is not available from your local video shop, which is usually the quickest and cheapest way to view it, the London office should also be able to get you a VHS copy.

Transferring Archive Film

News archive film is less of a problem as regards copyright fees, but be prepared for a large bill from American companies. Always see if the same event was covered by a British unit before you use American footage. Remember also that many film libraries charge a viewing fee for each roll of film you watch, even if it's not used. Some libraries may only have a negative of a clip you want to see and you'll have to pay for a print to be made, again whether it's used or not.

Having found your archive film, your troubles are not over. The usual way of compiling programmes which use a lot of archive film is to transfer the film on to videotape using a telecine machine, then make a film recording copy which is used for editing. The archive sequences on the master video tape are finally 'painted in' on a tape copy of the original show print, which contains any specially shot film, e.g. interviews.

Most film is on 35mm or 16mm stock but there are other gauges used by amateurs including Super 8mm (the current domestic format), Standard 8mm and, very rarely, 9.5mm. The situation is further complicated by two important forms of archive 35mm that you must take account of. Silent 35mm (pre 1930s) has a larger visible frame area than its modern counterpart and, if projected on modern equipment, a strip of picture on the left hand side is lost. This is particularly obvious on intertitles, the 'story cards' included in all silent films to explain the more obscure parts of the plot. If you can tolerate the loss of picture and/or you don't need the intertitles then make no special arrangements. If you need to see the whole frame, then you must ensure that the telecine is fitted with a silent 35mm gate facility.

Nitrate 35mm was phased out in approximately 1953 when it was replaced by Safety 35mm stock. Films made on this nitrate base are highly inflammable and, in time, disintegrate into an explosive jelly. Special safety precautions must be observed when using nitrate and these vary depending on local regulations governing the place you view/transfer it.

NEVER accept 35mm nitrate film or even a can that could contain such film (e.g. film found in an attic or other non-professional archive) without advice from an archive specialist.

NEVER bring uninspected nitrate on to any BBC premises or to any external facilities company.

For BBC use, all nitrate must be examined by arrangement with the Projection and Editing Servicing Manager, Television Film Studios, unless it is supplied by the Imperial War Museum, Pathe or British Movietone.

Facilities for transferring all the above film formats including nitrate, but excluding 9.5mm, are available within the BBC. Outside facilities can handle all formats but note that 9.5mm is transferred by pointing an archive projector at a screen and videoing it with domestic quality equipment!

Films in all current formats are shot at 24 or 25 frames per second (FPS). For optimum quality these are all transferred at 25 FPS. Archive film can run at other speeds and the very earliest film didn't even necessarily run at a uniform speed: it was manually cranked round by the cameraman. To transfer these non-standard speed films, the BBC has telecines that run at 16 2/3 and 18 FPS. These give reasonable results for all but the most critical material. If other speeds are required there are two approaches. Either use a 'Varispeed' telecine, available outside the BBC for speeds between 8 and 32 FPS, or transfer the film to VT at 25 FPS and use a variable speed VT machine to copy off a corrected version. This second option is more flexible in that the latest VTs can replay at any speed between −1 and +3 times normal speed and you also retain the ability to change your mind and repeat the process without reacquiring the film. It is not possible to change the speed of a clip transferred at any speed other than 25 FPS without introducing unacceptable movement judder.

Independent facility houses are listed in two publications, *The Broadcast Production Guide* and *The Knowledge,* and it's mainly a question of ringing round with your particular problem and seeing who has the equipment to solve it. You can also apply to use the BBC's facilities, but you have to accept that its own productions have priority.

Another piece of technical gadgetry which is worth bearing in mind is the XY zoom. This is a device which allows zooming in on part of a film as it is being run through the machine. If, for example, you have a crowd scene and want to zoom in on part of it, or even one face, then this is the facility you need. It's a fairly standard piece of equipment which many companies have.

Videotape

Up to 1967 broadcast VT used 405 lines and, if you want to use an early programme that only exists on videotape, you will have to get this transferred to 625 lines. Another technical problem the researcher should be aware of, when working with VT, is the differing formats used in other countries. The USA and Japan have a system called NTSC (unkindly known as Never Twice the Same Colour) while Britain uses PAL and other countries PAL or SECAM. If you need to view cassette tapes made in countries using a different format, you'll either have to get them converted or watch them on a machine which can adapt between the formats. Almost certainly your video at home won't have this facility.

Chapter 5

Finding Locations

This is mainly the director's problem or, in the case of drama, the production manager's. As the researcher, you may well have to do some preliminary research on an area before filming begins, especially if you are going abroad. In this country there are a number of companies which specialise in finding locations, but these are obviously mainly used for drama production where, for example, a director may request a medieval castle, a waterfall and a harbour in which to film a caique, all in close proximity.

In documentaries, what you are filming generally dictates where it will be filmed but if, for example, you are doing a reconstruction of past events, you will have to look for locations that are, or can be made to look, like former times. Actually, you don't have to go very far back in time to be obliged to do this. One director doing something about the Troubles in Northern Ireland reconstructed a riot in Leeds because he thought that if he filmed it in Ireland there was a serious danger of the locals joining in.

For filming purposes if you're doing a long sequence, it's usually better to get somewhere which is not occupied at the moment, e.g. a disused railway station, a row of houses awaiting clearance or an old factory which is going to be demolished. The cost of dressing such a place is usually less than it would be to pay people to stay away or interrupt filming frequently while the ordinary business of the place goes on. But do get a safety officer to check out the building first.

Make sure that the owners of the property know exactly what you intend to do and the size of the film crew. Reassure them about insurance cover and that the place will be cleaned up and restored to its original condition when you leave. If the owner is at all unwilling, get somewhere else. It will all end in tears otherwise. If you're going to be there for some time or you need any special co-operation, e.g. night shoots or closing off a street, talk to the neighbours as well and make sure they are, if not ecstatic, reasonably happy. Most people like the idea of having a film crew around, but they rarely realise how disruptive it can be. Tell them.

Expense is one of the major problems of location filming. The director may be all agog with the visual potential of a castle or a stately home, but find out early on how much all this is going to cost and what hidden extras there may be. The daily rate to hire a place may seem low, but do you also have to pay for security personnel in addition? And how about insurance? All production crews must have insurance, but the rate may be prohibitively high if you are planning to film where there is the possibility of doing expensive damage. If you are using a suburban home and a Green Lady from Woolworths has a lamp fall on it, the bill is going to be a lot lower than if a cameraman's boot goes through Lord Snooks' Gainsborough. This, in turn, will affect the amount of cover the production will have to take out.

Even if the director decides to film in what looks like a public place, things may still not be simple. Many public places are, in fact, private property, e.g. the Royal Parks in London or even Trafalgar Square, which is owned by the Crown. Not a lot of people know that. Shopping centres, which always look a good bet for vox pops, being free of traffic noise and protected from the weather, are nearly always privately owned. Those that aren't are subject to the local council and either way permission must be granted to film there. Whether getting permission to film is the researcher's responsibility or the production assistant's depends on how your team works. What is important is that somebody does it. Start off with the local authority; if they don't own the site they will know who does, since they collect community charges.

Make sure also that someone has sorted out police permission to film in any public place. There is a set of regulations about what film crews may or may not do and when they may do it, quite apart from the owner of land's permission. By and large, you can forget extensive street filming in the centre of London, but most other places are more amenable if given notice and detailed information. In large cities you will be dealing with inspectors, or even chief inspectors, who have other major concerns — allow time to get permission.

The Recce

Once you and the production assistant have steered your enthusiastic director away from the budget-breaking location envisaged to somewhere cheaper, you still have to sort out the recce. Before you go, get a large-scale Ordnance Survey map of the area and a reasonably detailed road map on a smaller scale. Check both maps carefully for potentially disruptive elements. Airfields are an obvious hazard but schools, unless you are filming in the holidays, can be a nuisance. Not only will there be a lot of noise as the children arrive and leave, but during playtime or games lessons you'd be amazed at the decibel level. I speak as one who lives a street away from a modest-sized primary school. Also find out what any factory does — drop forges and buzz saws produce a sound that, on a clear day, can carry a surprising distance. Transmitter stations, which can seriously disrupt electronics, military and radar installations can all play merry hell with radio mikes and video recording systems, although film is less of a problem, in their vicinity.

It's one of the lesser-known laws of the universe that recces always present the acceptable face of location filming. Noisy building sites and street repairs are miraculously suspended, traffic where you are planning to film in the street is always lighter than usual and the weather is the best since records began. Recce on the same day of the week you intend to film. Do check if anything special is planned for the day of your filming. Is there going to be a parade through the streets or demonstration of some description? Or, if filming in the country, a car rally or funfair? This sort of information should be available either in the local library, where forthcoming attractions will be on the noticeboard, or from the police, because they will be involved in any street activity.

If the director is young and innocent, paint the worst possible scenario. The cameraman should do this for you, as a breed they have seen it all before and tend to be cynical, but if you can't recce with the cameraman, the researcher must play Cassandra to the director's Candide.

Also on the recce, and this is in your own interest, check out places for lunch, hotels where the production team can stay, even things like garages if you are filming in the back of beyond. Hospitals, emergency dentists (what are you going to do if your reporter's front crowns fall off after biting into the local cuisine?), the nearest railway station or airport, vets (if you're using animals) and local taxi firms should all be noted. If filming in town, where are you going to park?

On the day of the filming arrive early and with the director check out the location. Things may have changed since the recce and you'll need time to come up with alternatives if the local council has decided to dig up the road in front of the building where you intend to film. If you are only doing a brief sequence, a judiciously applied fiver might be enough to hold up roadworks while the filming is completed.

If you're interviewing someone in his or her office or home, have a close look at what will be appearing in the background. I don't just mean taking down pictures whose glass might reflect the crew — that's the kind of thing the cameraman should notice — but even smaller detail. For example, a lot of people like to appear against their bookcase to show what cultured, intellectual types they are. Disgruntled secretaries or spouses have been known to rearrange books so that a campaigner for stricter moral values is filmed with the *Kama Sutra* placed behind the left ear, or a distinguished novelist undermines any claim to literary eminence by appearing with a well-thumbed copy of the latest bodice-ripper prominently displayed.

Filming Abroad

Location filming in this country is bad enough but going abroad is even worse. It really needs a book to itself. Most of the time you'll be going to countries which aren't so different from this one and whose tapwater is probably a sight healthier. The following is largely about the parts of the globe that make you glad to come home.

The best and most up-to-date information comes from people who have just returned from filming in the country you are going to. They will enjoy freezing your blood and re-living all those incidents which are so nightmarish to live through and so hilarious in retrospect. They can also advise you on fixers and translators, although in some countries these will be arranged through the Ministry of Information or Culture and you will be given no choice in the matter.

The country's embassy or high commission in London will be able to give you some information but, as they are essentially involved in a PR exercise, they may not mention all the little quirks that make their country so, how shall I put it, interesting to work in. Some years ago I was talking to a production assistant on *Chronicle* who was going off to a foreign country for a month's filming. I was deeply envious of her luck, but when I saw her on her return was surprised to find her complexion as pale and interesting as when she departed. She explained she had seen very little of the country, or indeed of the filming: almost the entire four weeks had been spent in the Customs shed bribing officials to get the equipment and luggage in and then the film out. This is not the sort of local detail you can expect the embassy or high commission to supply.

What they can tell you are the requirements for visas and inoculation certificates. Some countries take longer to issue visas than others. Although film crews are usually well prepared for foreign travel, check that anyone in the team from, say, Australia or New Zealand or even the Irish Republic has made the appropriate arrangements, since these may vary from those applying to British citizens. A company in London, the Visa Shop, can arrange and collect them for you if you haven't time to queue at the relevant embassies. Information about inoculation certificates can also be obtained from the DHSS's International Relations branch. Your local DHSS office can tell you about arrangements for free medical care in other European Community countries. The World Health Organisation sends out regular bulletins about outbreaks of disease in different countries which your own doctor or health centre should have.

You may not be officially required to have a polio jab before entering a country but if the WHO bulletin says there's an epidemic of it there, you'd be mad not to have a booster or whatever. Also check your route. You may not need a certificate for, say, yellow fever for your final destination, but if you land in another country *en route* you may need it there.

Apart from the problems of disease, there are other life-threatening situations to take into consideration. You don't have to go further than Northern Ireland to recognise that political factors are something a good researcher should find out about before departure. Read the papers assiduously and see if you can get access to Reuters and the Press Association reports. These need interpreting; local correspondents and stringers may have a better insight into what's going on but, as they live there, they also need to temper their reports with enough discretion to make sure they aren't ignominiously expelled or worse. The Foreign and Commonwealth Office will also give *ad hoc* advice.

Paying due respect to the customs of another culture is obviously a Good Thing so find out what you should and shouldn't do. Everyone knows that cows in India are sacred but there are a million other tiny nuances of behaviour and gesture that you should be aware of before you land in Oman, Osaka or even Oslo and start offending local sensibilities. Information of this kind would come either from natives of the country or from language schools that run short courses for business travellers to give an introduction to a language and culture.

Make sure you also know about public holidays. If you arrive on a bank holiday you may find it difficult to change money and to contact officials or other people vital to your filming. If you are going to a Muslim country, check that you will not be arriving there during Ramadan. Filming then can be something of a strain as the fasting observed by all good Muslims during the day tends to lower the stamina and shorten the temper of all concerned. Find out what the attitude to alcohol is before you go. Some states are totally dry, while others turn a blind eye to foreigners drinking so long as they do it very discreetly.

The weather is another important factor, especially in countries affected by monsoons. Extremes of temperature and humidity can damage film stock, videotape and equipment so, unless you absolutely have to, going in the wettest or hottest months of the year is counter-productive. Also find out about night-time temperatures. Some places are blazingly hot during the day, but at night the temperature falls sharply. Make sure you're suitably equipped for both extremes.

British driving licences or international licences, which can be obtained from the AA or RAC, are recognised throughout most of the world. Some places may, however, require you to take a driving test if you are staying longer than a few weeks. Generally speaking you are best advised to get a local driver — this is especially important in some countries where killing a chicken may count as a lynching offence. You haven't got time to research traffic regulations in Ulan Bator or wherever, so get someone who knows about them from first-hand knowledge and anyway is used to the driving conditions. Greek and Spanish traffic laws have their, to us, funny little quirks about responsibility in case of accident. It sounds callous, but make sure that if anything does go wrong, it's not you or the director who's in jail during the editing period. Hire a local driver.

Chapter 6

Finding Sound

Music and sound effects are largely the province of the director and film or VT editor, who will choose any music needed in the background of a sequence and lay any sound effects necessary at the dub. You may, however, be asked to find a selection of the kind of music wanted or to track down any particularly unusual sound effect.

While I was working on a documentary about the Duke and Duchess of Windsor, we found a clip of archive film from the 1920's showing the Duke, when Prince of Wales, touring Africa. A group of local musicians and dancers were laying on the kind of show still thought suitable to entertain royalty. Drummers drummed, pipers piped and bare-breasted ladies leaped. Unfortunately the commentary, which the director did not want, was on the same track as the music and the two could not be separated. I started to investigate experts on African music who could identify the instruments being used and recordings of music they could be playing. In the event, there wasn't the money to pay an expert and to hire musicians to duplicate the music. As there were so many close-ups of the instruments being played, we realised that no record could match sound and picture. People would have to be brought in specially to make a complete new sound track for the clip. We finally decided the sequence was too short and occupied too small a place in the whole programme to justify the expense.

In this case, it was music that had to be reconstructed from visual clues only. More frequently, you will find that it is a sound effect that is missing. The director should get any necessary sound, either sync or as a wild track, while filming. Occasionally this will not be possible. Other sounds might have drowned the one you are trying to emphasise or the subject may have been shot on a very long lens, so to all intents and purposes the film is mute.

The director may also want to re-lay a noise that does not come up to expectations. Real gunshots, for example, sound feeble to an audience used to Hollywood extravaganza. It is essential to make sure that you get the right sound effect. Dubbing theatres have a full library of effects on disc, which are played in at the right moment, but carelessness can cause a flood of letters from the viewing public. This is particularly common on news programmes; when time is at a premium the temptation to snatch a disc, any disc with approximately the right noise, is great. Even *John Craven's Newsround* has a critical audience who, though still at primary school, can tell the sound of a DC10 taking off from that of a 707. A little research will prevent such errors.

The library of effects discs in the dubbing theatre would certainly have contained the right sound. The catalogue of effects available on BBC discs alone runs to three hundred-and-ninety-eight closely printed pages, encompassing sounds from Abbeys to Zoos. A browse through a catalogue if you have an hour or so is both amusing and instructive. You can get twenty-six seconds of a goldfish squealing in water (in captivity) should you ever need it.

If you do have something even more unusual, however, it's no use turning up at the dubbing theatre with footage of a rare South American bird and saying 'Can we have some sound on that, please?' Even if you are lucky enough to have a dubbing mixer whose hobby is ornithology and who recognises the lesser spotted Butzenheimer's Shrike, it's unlikely that its call will be anywhere on a standard effects disc. Get your research done before you go; identify the bird, look in an effects catalogue or check with the dubbing theatre if its call is on disc and, if it isn't, make sure that you have the sound from another source.

Copyright

Theoretically, sound effects are copyrighted but in practice I suspect most people ignore this. A tray of crockery being dropped sounds much the same whoever happens to have recorded it. Music is an entirely different problem and the pitfalls that can befall someone who has no knowledge of the problems of music copyright are legion.

What they all boil down to is that there are only a very limited number of commercial records that can be used and the right to use them must be negotiated and cleared in advance. Life is much easier if your company has a specific department to deal with this. If not, you can ask the Mechanical Copyright Protection Society to act as negotiator with the owner(s) of the rights to a specific recording. There is no fixed scale of fees; the amount charged will depend on how the music is to be used, whether you expect a peak-time audience on network television or you are making a community video you expect only a small number of people to see and whether you will be selling your programme abroad. This last is the major factor; getting world rights to a commercial record is horrendously difficult.

Your director might ask you to find a selection of eighteenth century music to accompany a stills sequence of architectural drawings. On the face of it, this looks quite simple. From a history of music, you gather a number of names and armed with this go to a record library or shop and get a pile of discs to listen to. (S)he then picks something that will be suitable. If you find that the record chosen cannot be cleared, you have two alternatives. You can book a group of musicians to record exactly the music you want or you can go for mood music.

Mood Music

A number of companies produce records of all kinds of music from ethnic folk to pieces in the style of Mozart, Chopin, Debussy, etc. There are also shorter items like trumpet fanfares, musical stings and background music suitable for every kind of scene, pastoral, threatening, humorous, etc.

Mood music has a number of advantages besides the fact that it can be cleared for copyright with no problems at all, although it must still be paid for, and world rights may prove very expensive. To take our eighteenth century example, if your director does choose an authentic piece by Mozart or Albinoni, you'll probably find that the time taken to develop a musical idea is much longer than the sequence needs. In addition, Mozart's music is notoriously difficult to edit. His modulations are so subtle that they often escape notice until you try and edit the opening statement to a later passage. If you choose mood music 'in the style of Mozart', you'll get a short, self-contained piece that will sound like his work but will not present too many editing difficulties.

Aesthetically, however, mood music tends to be bland and undistinguished. If you have ever watched a particular kind of promotional video, you will have heard mood music. You will know that its injudicious use can make even the most exciting pictures seem dull and soporific. This is not to say, don't use mood music, just explore other options first and, in any case, employ it sparingly.

Period Music

At this point, the director adds a further complication by deciding to go for authentic period instruments. This will almost certainly mean hiring musicians. Although the mood music companies do include pieces from the popular classics, Beethoven's Ninth, Schubert's Trout Quintet, etc., there is very, very little on fortepiano or clavichord. On *Vanity Fair: The Battlefield*, a training film about the visual effects used in the making of the BBC Drama series, the director toyed with the idea of using period instruments.

I made a list of tunes played during the time of the Napoleonic Wars by both the French and English but the only versions on record or in the BBC's Sound Archives were by modern military bands and they just sounded wrong. Using a bit of lateral thinking, I discovered that there is a Napoleonic Association, a group of men dedicated to restaging battles of the period. I rang their chairman who confirmed that they did have a band with authentic instruments. Only the fact that the band was based in Belgium stopped us hiring them for a recording session. How often are our best artistic endeavours defeated by monetary considerations! In the end, we settled for a modern piece by the Moody Blues (which took our experts in the copyright department three months to clear and licence) and hired one person to record some drum taps.

Music is perhaps the best method of establishing a mood and if it is set in the context of a radio programme will instantly evoke an era. *ITMA* tells the viewer this is wartime, *Housewives Choice* fifties and sixties suburbia and pirate radio that we are in the Swinging London of the late sixties. This last example presents a bit of a copyright problem. As pirate radio is by definition illegal, the question of who actually owns the copyright of the DJ's links (no problem about the music being played) is a knotty one. When in doubt, talk to your lawyers and test it in court if the director is feeling brave and you have the money.

Where you get recordings of pirate radio is another matter. I worked on an amateur production of a play set in Swinging London and one of those connected with it had been working in mainstream radio at the time. He had, however, made a number of recordings of historic events among which he included pieces from Radio Caroline, Radio London and other lesser pirate radio stations, rightly recognising that these would be of interest in the future.

Those with a professional interest in a medium often take and keep recordings of interest, not only radio and television broadcasts, but also farewell concerts of singers and musicians. Tracking them down is a matter of patient tele-phoning and advertising in appropriate journals. Alternatively, the director will just have to fake it.

The British Library National Sound Archive

The major source of recorded sound in this country is the National Sound Archive, which is now part of the British Library.

Its major sections are music (classical, popular, jazz, traditional); the spoken word (literature, documentary, language and dialect, oral history); wildlife sounds (some sixty-thousand recordings principally of birds and mammals) and industrial-mechanical sound. It also has copies of much of the BBC's Sound Archives and Transcription Service material, including stuff that was junked by the BBC in one of its fits of corporate madness.

Researchers who use the National Sound Archive should telephone first to ascertain whether the material they want is available and to make an appointment to use the listening facilities. One of the problems is that cataloguing of the holdings is not complete, so knowledge of what material is actually held often depends on the staff of each section, but an extensive reference library is available to researchers. A search and transcription service operates to track down an item and make a copy of it, but permission for a recording to be used must be obtained from the copyright holder (if one exists) by the researcher. Charges are made for use of the service.

There are a number of services and publications of great use to the television researcher. *The Directory of Recorded Sound Sources* (though pricey) is an excellent guide to collections of both private and commercial recordings in this country. *POMPI* (the Popular Music Periodicals Index) is an annual publication indexing articles from ninety periodicals about pop and jazz. The National Discography, at present only available at the National Sound Archive or the MCPS, is a data base of commercial records.

Although the Sound Archive does not have an extensive collection of the actual means of reproducing sound, e.g. early models of record players, tape recorders or whatever, it does have some that can be examined to make a reproduction for, say, an historical reconstruction, and photographs may be available.

Their technical expertise is considerable. Recently a film company found some wire recordings (an early form of dictaphone) made by Jung which they wanted to get transferred in order to be able to use in a programme about the eminent psychiatrist and this was accomplished without actually having to track down and use the original machinery of the wire recorder.

A particularly interesting and useful piece of equipment currently in development is CEDAR (Computer Enhanced Digital Audio Restoration). You the researcher have managed to find a record of great rarity but unfortunately it is badly scratched. Or you have a reel of com-opt film on which the part carrying the sound is damaged.

CEDAR listens to the sound and, instead of just cutting out the noise of the click or damaged section with the inevitable distortion this produces, listens to what went before the offending part, what went after and comes up with what happened in the middle where the damage is. A new, clean and authentic recording of the music or whatever can thus be made. It will also work for cylinders and magnetic tape. An explanatory leaflet for those of a technical bent, and further information on access to CEDAR, is available.

Chapter 7

Keeping Records

The method you choose to keep records of what you are researching is really up to you but, whichever one you do decide on, make sure that it will allow you to retrieve material easily and accurately.

For rough notes of 'phone calls and copying out information from printed sources I use a large, bound notebook. Envelopes get lost, loose leaf and spiral-bound books lose pages — they either fall out or someone else in the office writes a message or a telephone number on a page and then rips it out, taking vital information written on the other side with it. For some psychological reason, your colleagues don't do this to a bound notebook and neither do you.

Try to date everything, even if it's only at the top of a page, so you can work out when you spoke to someone. This is the counsel of perfection — I've never done it consistently in my life but when I haven't it's often been vital to know when one particular telephone conversation took place. Likewise, note the name of a publication and its date for information copied from books, newspapers or journals. If you're using records from the Public Record Office or the British Library, note the piece number or shelf-mark in case you have to go back to check or expand your notes.

It's also worth noting everything you have looked at, even if there was no information to record: this is especially important on a long-term project. You might find yourself several months later getting a sense of *déjà-vu* and realising you've already read this source, but it yielded nothing worthwhile.

From these rough notes, type out the salient points for the director and keep a copy or two for yourself. These I put into a folder, along with photocopies of material that seems relevant.

As a former secretary I can theoretically take shorthand and I do use it to take notes of telephone conversations. But if I don't type them up immediately, I can rarely read them back. Unless you're court reporter standard, don't trust shorthand, especially if you might need to refer to your notes months later.

For some programmes, an index card system is useful. You can either arrange it by subject, e.g. housing, agriculture, crime, if you're doing something on social conditions in the thirties, or chronologically, if you're doing a biography or a series of closely interlinked events, like the causes of the First World War or the progress of a computer fraud. A brief abstract of the information and a note of the source is all that's needed. The series *Our House*, which was six thirty-minute programmes about people who had lived in the same house for over fifty years, interviewed hundreds of families before selecting the final six. Names, addresses and brief notes about all the houses and people seen were kept in a card index, in case one family had to drop out before filming began.

Computers and the Law

If you're computer literate, this kind of information can be put on disc. Always make backup copies. It's also a good idea to make sure that other people in the office can use the computer or, if you have one at home, that at least one other person understands the system you are using. If you fall under a number nine bus with the meaning of life definitively worked out, but stored in such a way that no-one knows how to retrieve it, what will happen to your posthumous place in the history books? Or, more importantly, to the programme?

The other disadvantage of computers is that you might fall foul of the Data Protection Act (1984) if you use your computer to store information about people. Your organisation or even you if you have a home computer, must be registered and people have the right of access to what you have stored about them. You may run into problems (this act has yet to be tested in court) if you have notes about an interview to which you have appended opinions of the interviewee. Even if these are for your eyes only, the said expert, boring, long-winded and useless though you may consider him, has a right to see your notes, but only if they are kept on computer — index cards and pieces of paper in a folder are exempt from this law.

If you use a cassette machine to tape record interviews you should use a separate tape for each interview and make a verbal identification at the beginning, i.e. the name of the interviewee, your name and the date plus any other relevant information necessary for that particular interview. Write on the outside of the tape the name of the interviewee. Keep these tapes until a long, long time after transmission if there is any chance at all of a dispute about what was said. You may, for example, use information given to you at an interview in the commentary, rather than filming the person speaking, and then have to prove that you were given those facts. This is especially important if the subject of the programme is at all controversial. It's a wise precaution when dealing with contentious issues to tape record all interviews and not to rely on your notes or recollection of events alone.

Presentation

At the end of your research gathering, you will have pages of notes, lists of stills and film clips with their whereabouts, piles of tapes and transcriptions and your desk will probably also be cluttered with overdue library books, photocopies of press cuttings, VHS tapes of other programmes with possibly useful footage and several scraps of paper with mysterious telephone numbers on. You will not be wonderfully popular if you gather them all up and transfer them to the director's desk.

What (s)he wants is a typed summary of the information and sources available. How much detail you need to include will depend on your director's particular way of working and how much time you have had to discuss the progress of the work. On a long-term project you should always keep the director informed about what you are doing, so you will have conversations about the research and will know which parts are of particular interest and value. If you are doing a magazine item, although the amount of information will be less, the editor will need much closer detail since there will probably not have been time for a long discussion, or indeed for any discussion at all.

Chapter 8

The Aftermath

A film is not finished until it is transmitted. While you are working on a programme, you'll probably get so caught up in it that it's your last thought on most nights and your first in the morning. It's easy to forget that the end result is something that could be seen by a potential audience of millions. How do you let all those people out there know what they might otherwise miss?

Publicity

Most companies have a publicity department who will take more or less kindly to offers of help from the production team. If they are busy launching a series that is taking up most of their time, they might welcome your offer to do the publicising yourself. As a researcher, you can make a list of publications that will be interested in your programme and might give you a plug. Local papers should not be despised: if you used their advertising columns to find people to contribute, ringing them up to tell them who was found through their pages should guarantee you a good half-page article. Likewise, if you filmed in their area you'll probably get a mention. Ditto local radio.

The invaluable *Willings' Press Guide* will list suitable journals and magazines. This kind of publicity should be started well in advance, as the press date will probably be several weeks before the publication date.

Finding the right angle to approach a publication is essential and a carefully worded letter to a named individual will produce better results than a photocopied press release. In these days of word processors, this is easy to achieve.

If you are having a press preview, find out as far as possible whether anyone else is previewing on the same day. If a rival company is launching a glamorous spy-drama and laying on champagne and nibbles in the presence of the stars of the show, you'd be unlikely to attract the newspaper hacks with offers of instant coffee and a packet of chocolate digestives. Choose a day when the alternative seems much less exciting than your programme, or arrange for a tape to be sent to the individual previewers. This often works out cheaper than booking a viewing theatre if only two or three journalists turn up.

In the course of your research, you will have spoken to a number of people who should be informed of the date of transmission, either because they have expressed an interest in knowing or because they have been filmed and then either included or dropped from the final programme. The production assistant should have a list of those filmed and it will probably be her responsibility to send letters to them.

The really well-organised will have passed names to the production assistant during the course of research for inclusion on the list of those to be contacted. Foolish virgins will spend a lot of time turning the pages of notebooks and looking through diaries in the hope of being reminded just who else wants to know. You cannot afford to lose any part of your potential audience so learn to be well organised.

Tidying Up

Any material borrowed from whatever source needs to be returned. Pictures from agencies, books from libraries, rare records from sound collections will all be prominently labelled with the owner's name. Problems arise when you get things from private sources, family snapshots or books that contributors have loaned. Immediately you are given something, as personally valuable as private photographs, put them in a cardboard-backed envelope to protect them and label them. You may think you'll remember where you borrowed something but two or three months and a pile of other objects later and you'll have forgotten just who the lady in the pince-nez and bustle is.

Although your production's insurance should cover losses of this kind, most people don't want the money, they want their picture of Great-Aunt Fanny or the book, now out-of-print, from which you took stills of steam locomotives. If, after an exhaustive search, the photo or the book cannot be found, do your best to replace it. If the photograph was used in the programme, get a blow-up of it from the film (the quality will not be wonderful, but it will be better than nothing). The copy made while doing rostrum camera work, if any was done, might also be acceptable.

For lost books, there are a number of people who specialise in tracking down out-of-print works. Their charges (as I know from experience) are surprisingly low, especially if the book is of no antiquarian value. They advertise in the specialist press, e.g. *The Book Collector,* and in some literary journals. All this might seem just too much like hard work when you are in the thick of setting up another project but good PR is never wasted. You simply never know when you will need someone's help again and a good general motto for researchers is *Ni Nisi De Amicis Bonum*, which, freely translated, means Never Alienate a Possible Contact.

Chapter 9

Addresses &
Reference Books

Part II

The following addresses are only intended as a starting point. Since literally anything can be the basis of a programme or item, it would be impossible to include every single organisation that a researcher might at any time in the future wish to contact. I have therefore concentrated on the main organisations in each area but have also included a number of smaller agencies and associations which seem to me the most potentially useful. For national groups I have given the HQ only, but you should be able to get local branches from them.

In compiling this section, I have divided up the addresses according to subject matter. This seemed to me a more sensible arrangement than putting them into Societies, Trade Associations, Self-Help Groups, etc. Thus the League Against Cruel Sports is included in Sport & Recreation because, doing an item on hunting, you would want to represent the views of both sides. This system has the added advantage that in running your eye down all the addresses in one section, you might well see something new that will give you an idea for an angle on your story that might not have been immediately apparent.

This method does have disadvantages. I have included organisations in the area where they seem to me most likely to be used. For example, the Historic Houses Association is included under Locations because they will most often be useful in finding a nice little Georgian farmhouse in which to film, but a researcher doing an item on government grants for listed buildings would find them a source of both information and case histories. I could, of course, have listed the Association in two sections but cross-referencing every organisation in every section where it might be remotely useful would be impossible. Finding your way round the addresses will be an interesting exercise in lateral thinking. Here are a few clues to help you: specialist libraries are listed under Facts but museums appear under the relevant subject. All ministries come under Government & Politics.

The Freemasons gave me a lot of trouble. Should they appear in Sport & Recreation, Business, Commerce & Industry or even

Family and Social Welfare since they lay heavy emphasis on their charity work? I even toyed with the idea of creating an Odds & Sods section but in the end put them under Religion & Beliefs which will no doubt infuriate Grand Masters of Lodges all over the country.

There is also a problem with small groups, especially self-help ones. They tend to change personnel and addresses quite frequently or even go out of business, if funding dries up. You should be able to find a telephone number of a small group from another in a related area. For example, the National Association for Maternal & Child Welfare will know about the various support groups for parents of stillborn children, single parents, etc.

People also tend to know about the opposition. You can often kill two birds with one stone by asking one organisation where to contact the pressure group opposing them. In many cases they will co-operate, but don't rely on it. When the Abbey National wanted to become a limited company, its information office putting the case for the change refused to divulge any information about the opposition. And I know from experience that the press offices of government ministries can display an apparent lack of knowledge which might make the uncharitable wonder if their intelligence-gathering is all the taxpayer might expect.

If all else fails, a glance through the telephone directory can be helpful. Most large organisations have their headquarters in London so a trawl through (National) Association of..., Institute of..., (Royal) Society for... or Commission on... can at least give you a starting point.

At the beginning of each section is a list of reference books with the most useful marked by an asterisk. If you work regularly in a particular area of programmes, it might be worth your while acquiring them. In any case, you should have access to the following standard reference works, all of which and many more will be available in your local library if your company doesn't have them:

Standard dictionaries, e.g. Oxford, Chambers, Websters (for American usage)

Encyclopaedia Britannica

Guinness Book of Records

Dictionaries of Quotations

Good atlas of the world, e.g. Times

Who's Who

Willings Press Guide

Pears Cyclopaedia

DISCLAIMER: Inclusion in the following list of addresses does not necessarily imply approval, nor is it a guarantee of quality.

nimals &
omestic Pets

blications:

**:imek's Animal Life
:yclopedia** (13 volumes)
.n Nostrand Reinhold
npany, New York, 1972)
orms of life from the
plest one-celled organisms
lan described in detail with
itat, etc.

dresses:

imal Health Trust
atone Lodge
Newmarket
ailwell Road
folk CB8 7DW
38) 661111
arity concerned with all
ects of veterinary medicine;
ensive research
grammes, some of which
e applications in human
dicine.

**imal Virus Research
stitute**
n Road
bright
king
rrey GU24 0NF
-83) 232441

sociation of Aquarists
unty House
ardown
teley Hatch
singstoke
nts RG27 9JS
?56) 465461

itish Rabbit Council
refoy House
Kirkgate
wark
tts NG24 1AD
:36) 76042
verning body for showing
bits.

**British Veterinary
Association**
7 Mansfield Street
London W1M 0AT
(071) 636 6541

Cats Protection League
17 Kings Road
Horsham
West Sussex RH13 5PP
(0403) 65566

The Donkey Sanctuary
Sidmouth
Devon EX10 0NU
(0395) 578222
International donkey protection
trust.

Fancy Fowl
Crondall Cottage
Andover Road
Highclere
Newbury
Berks RG15 9PH
(0635) 253239
Specialist magazine for owners
and exhibitors of rare breeds of
chickens, geese, ducks, etc.
Can provide contacts for
individual breeds.

Feline Advisory Bureau
235 Upper Richmond Road
London SW15 6SN
(081) 789 9553
Advises on health and disease
in cats, boarding cattery
services, etc.

FIDO
16 Jacob Well Mews
London W1H 6BD
Pressure group campaigning
against inconsiderate dog
owners.

**Governing Council of the
Cat Fancy**
4-6 Penelorlieu
Bridgwater
Somerset TA6 3PG
(0278) 427575
Governing body of the pedigree
cat-breeding world.

**International Council for
Bird Preservation**
32 Cambridge Road
Girton
Cambridge CB3 0PJ
(0223) 277318

**International League for
the Protection of Horses**
Hallfarm
Snetterton
Norwich NR16 2LR
(0953) 82682

The Kennel Club
1 Clarges Street
London W1Y 8AB
(071) 493 6651
Governing body of the pedigree
dog-breeding world.

**National Canine Defence
League**
1 Pratt Mews
London NW1 0AD
(071) 388 0137

The Parrot Society
108B Fenlake Road
Bedford MK42 0EU
(0234) 358922

**People's Dispensary for
Sick Animals**
Whitechapel Way
Priorslee
Telford
ShropshireTF2 9PQ
(0952) 290990
Charity providing free veterinary
treatment for sick and injured
animals.

**Royal Society for the
Prevention of Cruelty to
Animals (RSPCA)**
Causeway
Horsham
West Sussex RH12 1HG
(0403) 64181

University Federation for Animal Welfare
8 Hamilton Close
Potters Bar
Herts EN6 3QD
(0707) 58202

Urban Wildlife Group
Unit 213
Jubilee Trades Centre
130 Pershore Road
Birmingham B5 6ND
(021) 666 7474

World Parrot Trust
Parkside Park
Hayle
Cornwall TR27 4HY

World Society for the Protection of Animals
Park Place
10 Lawn Lane
London SW8 1UD
(071) 793 0540

Zoo Check
162 Boundaries Road
London SW12 8HG
(081) 682 1818
Charitable trust monitoring animals in zoos and promoting conservation of animals in the wild.

The Arts & Media

Publications:

Brad Advertiser & Agency List (pub. quarterly Maclaine Hunter Ltd)
Directory of advertising agencies and their campaigns.

Blue Book of British Broadcasting (pub. Tellex Monitors Ltd, Communications House, 210 Old Street, London EC1V 9UN, (071) 490 8018)
Lists TV, radio, cable and satellite contacts in U.K., producers, presenters and executives.

Index of English Literary Manuscripts ed. John Horden et al. (London: Mansell 1980-).
Lists, describes and locates about 50,000 literary manuscripts owned by public and private collections in the UK, Europe and America.

National Union Catalog of Manuscript Collections (Washington, D.C.: Library of Congress 1959-).
Location of letters, manuscripts and memorabilia in 95 public and private American libraries. Being put on to computer. There is also an index to personal names which makes searching easier.

The New Cambridge Bibliography of English Literature (pub. Cambridge)
5 volumes, chronological order, giving authors, their works and books written about them. Also general subjects, e.g. drama of the period.

Whitaker's Publishers in the U.K. and their Addresses (pub. annually J. Whitaker & Sons Ltd, 12 Dyott Street, London WC1A 1DF, (071) 836 8911

*Writers & Artists Yearbook (pub. annually by A & C Black)

Addresses:

Advertising Association
Abford House
15 Wilton Road
London SW1V INJ
(071) 828 2771

Advertising Standards Authority
Brook House
2-16 Torrington Place
London WC1E 7HN
(071) 580 5555

An Comann Leabhraichean (Gaelic Books Council)
Dept. of Celtic
University of Glasgow
Glasgow G12 8QQ
(041) 339 8855
Promotes books in Gaelic, awards grants to authors, commissions books and sets competitions.

Anglia Television Ltd
Anglia House
Norwich NR1 3JG
(0603) 615151

Association for Business Sponsorship of the Arts (ABSA)
Nutmeg House
60 Gainsford Street
Butlers Wharf
London SE1 2NY
(071) 378 8143
Charity offering information and advice to arts organisations seeking sponsorship.

Association of Art Historians
c/o Prints, Drawings & Paintings Collection
V&A Museum
South Kensington
London SW7 2RL
(071) 938 8500

Association of Cinematograph Television & Allied Technicians (ACTT)
111 Wardour Street
London W1V 4AY
(071) 437 8506

Association of Independent Producers (AIP)
162-170 Wardour Street
London W1V 4LA
(071) 437 7700

Association of Model Agents
The Clockhouse
St Catherine's Mews
London SW3 2PU
(071) 584 6466

Book Trust (formerly **the National Book League**)
45 East Hill
London SW18 2QZ
(081) 870 9055
Promotes books generally, also has a Book Help Service to help track down a particular book or suggest titles and administers various literary prizes, e.g. Booker.

Booksellers Association of GB and Ireland
Minster House
272 Vauxhall Bridge Road
London SW1V 1BA
(071) 834 5477

Border Television
Broadcasting House
Carlisle
Cumbria CA1 3NT
(0228) 25101

British Academy of Film & Television Arts
195 Piccadilly
London W1V 9LG
(071) 734 0022

British Actors Equity Association
8 Harley Street
London W1N 2AB
(071) 637 9311/(071) 636 6367

British Board of Film Classification
3 Soho Square
London W1V 5DE
(071) 439 7961

British Broadcasting Corporation (BBC)
Broadcasting House
Portland Place
London W1A 1AA
(071) 580 4468

British Music Hall Society
c/o Brodie & Middleton Ltd
68 Drury Lane
London WC2B 5SP
(071) 836 3289/3280

Broadcasting Complaints Commission
Grosvenor Gardens House
35 & 37 Grosvenor Gardens
London SW1W 0BS
(071) 630 1966

Broadcasting Standards Council
5-8 The Sanctuary
London SW1P 3JS
(071) 233 0401

British Telecom
60-68 St Thomas Street
London SE1 3QU
(071) 403 7600

Cable Television Association
Floor 5
Artillery House
Artillery Row
London SW1
(071) 222 2900

Trade association for the cable television industry.

Carlton Television
15 St George Street
Hanover Street
London W1R 9DE
(071) 499 8050

Central Television
Central House
Broad Street
Birmingham B1 2JP
(021) 643 9898

Channel Four Television
60 Charlotte Street
London W1P 2AX
(071) 631 4444

Channel Television (CTV)
Television Centre
Rouge Bouillon
St. Helier
Jersey JE2 3ZD
Channel Isles
(0534) 68999

Children's Film & Television Foundation
Elstree Studios
Shenley Road
Borehamwood
Herts WD6 1JG
(081) 953 1600

Contemporary Art Society
20 John Islip Street
London SW1P 4LL
(071) 821 5323
Promotes contemporary art and helps acquire work by living artists for gift to public galleries.

Crafts Council
1 Oxendon Street
London SW1Y 4AT
(071) 930 4811

Crime Writers Association
P.O. Box 17
Tring
Herts HP23 5LP
For professional writers either of crime fiction or about crime. Attempts to get a telephone number have defied detection.

Defence, Press & Broadcasting Committee
Room 2235
Ministry of Defence
Main Building
Whitehall
London SW1A 2HB
(071) 218 2206

Design and Artists Copyright Society Ltd (DACS)
St Mary's Clergy House
2 Whitechurch Lane
London E1 7QR

The Design Council
28 Haymarket
London SW1Y 4SU
(071) 839 8000

Design Museum
Butler's Wharf
Shad Thames
London SE1 2YD
(071) 407 6265

European Community Youth Orchestra
53 Sloane Street
London SW1X 9SW
(071) 235 7671

European Script Fund
21 Stephen Street
London W1P 1PL
Scheme established by the European Commission to support the development of film and television projects of European appeal.

Federation Against Copyright Theft (FACT)
7 Victory Business Centre
Worton Road
Isleworth
Middlesex TW7 6ER
(081) 568 6646
Organisation set up by the major video companies to combat pirate videos.

Grampian Television plc
Queen's Cross
Aberdeen
Scotland AB9 2XJ
(0224) 646464

Graeae
10 Woad Lane
Great Coates
Grimsby DN37 9NH
(0472) 883040
The only professional theatre company of disabled people in Britain.

Granada Television Ltd
Granada TV Centre
Quay Street
Manchester M60 9EA
(061) 832 7211

Horniman Museum
100 London Road
Forest Hill
London SE23 3PQ
(081) 699 1872
Ethnographical arts and crafts from all over the world. Also large natural history collection.

HTV Wales
Television Centre
Cardiff CF5 6XJ
(0222) 590590

HTV West
The Television Centre
Bath Road
Bristol BS4 3HG
(0272) 778366

Independent Programme Producers Association (IPPA)
50-51 Berwick Street
London W1V 4RD
(071) 439 7034

Independent Publishers Guild
25 Cambridge Road
Hampton
Middlesex TW12 2JL
(081) 979 0250

Independent Television Companies Association Ltd
Knighton House
56 Mortimer Street
London W1N 8AN
(071) 636 6866

Independent Television News Ltd (ITN)
200 Gray's Inn Road
London WC1X 8XZ
(071) 833 3000

The Independent Theatre Council
Unit 129 West
Westminster Business Square
Durham Street
London SE11 5JA
(071) 820 1712
Management association for small and middle-scale professional theatre companies Information service.

Institute of Amateur Cinematographers
63 Woodfield Lane
Ashtead
Surrey KT21 2BT
(03722) 76358

London Weekend Television (LWT)
South Bank Television Centre
Upper Ground
London SE1 9LT
(071) 620 1620

Meridien
8 Montague Close
London Bridge
London SE1 9RD
(071) 378 7898

Museum of the Moving Image (MOMI)
South Bank
Waterloo
London SE1 8XT
(071) 928 3535

**usicians Benevolent
und**
Ogle Street
ondon W1P 7LG
71) 636 4481

usicians Union (MU)
-62 Clapham Road
ondon SW9 0JJ
71) 582 5566

**ational Campaign for the
rts**
rancis House
rancis Street
ondon SW1P 1DE
71) 828 4448
dependent lobbying group
mmitted to making the arts, in
neral, a higher priority in
ducation and in broadcasting.

**ational Museum of
hotography, Film &
elevision**
rince's View
radford
orks BD5 0TR
274) 727488

**ational Union of
ournalists (NUJ)**
14 Gray's Inn Road
ondon WC1X 8DP
71) 278 7916

EN International
8 King Street
ondon WC2E 8JT
71) 379 7939
efends freedom of expression
r writers in all countries.

he Poetry Society
1 Earls Court Square
ondon SW5 9DE
71) 373 7861
71) 921 0664 (Library)

**ress Complaints
ommission**
Salisbury Square
ondon EC4Y 8AE
71) 353 1248

Publishers Association
19 Bedford Square
London WC1B 3HJ
(071) 580 6321-5

Puppet Centre Trust
Battersea Arts Centre
Lavender Hill
London SW11 5JT
(071) 228 5335
Charity to promote and develop
the art of puppetry.

Response
P.O. Box 8
Stonehouse
Gloucestershire GL10 2B
Organisation to help people
who think they are unfairly
treated by the press.

Reuters
85 Fleet Street
London EC4P 3AJ
(071) 250 1122

The Robert Opie Collection
Museum of Advertising and
Packaging
Albert Warehouse
Gloucester Docks
Gloucester GL1 2EH
(0452) 308507
Unique collection of packaging
and advertising material from
mid-1800s to present day.

Royal Academy of Arts
Burlington Arcade
Piccadilly
London W1V 0DS
(071) 439 7438

Royal Academy of Music
Marylebone Road
London NW1 5HT
(071) 935 5461

Royal Ballet School
155 Talgarth Road
London W14 9DE

The Royal Collection
Royal Library
Windsor Castle
Windsor
Berkshire SL4 1NJ

Royal College of Music
Prince Consort Road
London SW7 2BS
(071) 589 3643
Collection of portraits of
musicians and the largest
archive of concert programmes
in Great Britain.

**Royal Fine Arts
Commission**
7 St James's Square
London SW1Y 4JU
(071) 839 6537

**Royal Institute of British
Architects (RIBA)**
66 Portland Place
London W1N 4AD
(071) 580 5533

Royal Television Society
Tavistock House East
Tavistock Square
London WC1H 9HR
(071) 387 1970/1332

Scottish Museums Council
County House
20/22 Torphichen Street
Edinburgh EH3 8JB

Scottish Television plc
Cowcaddens
Glasgow G2 3PR
(041) 332 9999

**Sianel Pedwar Cymru
(S4C)**
Parc Ty Glas
Llanishen
Cardiff CF4 5DU
(0222) 747444

Sky Television plc
Grant Way
6 Centor Business Centre
Isleworth
Middx TW7 5QD
(071) 782 3000

Society of Authors
84 Drayton Gardens
London SW10 9SB
(071) 373 6642

Independent trade union which also administers a number of literary awards.

Society of Women Writers and Journalists
c/o Mary Reusten
13 Warwick Avenue
Cuffley
Herts EN6 4RU
(0707) 872311

Sunrise Television
The London Television Centre
London SE1 9LT
(071) 737 8995

Television South plc (TVS)
TV Centre
Northam
Southampton SO9 5HZ
(0703) 634211

Television South West (TSW)
Derry's Cross
Plymouth
Devon PL1 2SP
(0752) 663322

Thames Television Ltd
306-316 Euston Road
London NW1 3BB
(071) 387 9494

Theatre Museum
1E Tavistock Street
London WC2E 7PA
(071) 836 7891

TV-am
Breakfast Television Centre
Hawley Crescent
London NW1 8E
(071) 267 4300

Tyne Tees Television Ltd
The Television Centre
City Road
Newcastle-upon-Tyne
NE1 2AL
(091) 2610181

UK Cable Authority
Gillingham House
38 Gillingham Street
London SW1V 1HU
(071) 584 7011
Regulatory authority for cable television.

Ulster Television plc
Havelock House
Ormeau Road
Belfast
N. Ireland BT7 1EB
(0232) 328122

Welsh Books Council/Cyngor Llyfrau Cymraeg
Castell Brychan
Aberystwyth
Dyfed SY23 2JB
(0970) 624151

West Country Television
c\o Brittany Ferries
Millray Docks
Plymouth PL1 3EW
(0752) 253322

Women in Publishing
c/o J. Whitaker & Sons Ltd
12 Dyott Street
London WC1A 1DF
(071) 836 8911

The Writer's Guild of Great Britain
430 Edgware Road
London W2 1EH
(071) 723 8074

Yorkshire Television Ltd
The Television Centre
Leeds LS3 1JS
(0532) 438283

Business Commerce & Industry

Publications:
Croner's A-Z of Business Information Source
(pub. Croner Publications Croner House, London Road, Kingston-upon-Thames Surrey KT2 6BR
(081) 547 3100)
Loose-leaf reference book updated quarterly.

*The Times 1000 (pub. annually Times Books L
Details the top companies in each sector of commerce an in various overseas countries with financial statistics, directors and number of employees.

Who Owns Whom (pub. annually Dun & Bradstree
Different volumes cover the world: directory of companies and who owns them.

Addresses:
Advisory Conciliation ar Arbitration Service
27 Wilton Street
London SW1X 7AZ
(071) 210 3000

Association of Bankrup
4 Johnson Close
Abraham Heights
Lancaster LA1 5EU
(0524) 64305

Association of British Credit Unions
Unit 307
Westminster Business Square
339 Kennington Lane
London SE11 5QY
(071) 582 2626

**ssociation of British
surers**
dermary House
-15 Queen Street
ndon EC4N 1TT
71) 248 4477

**ssociation of Future
rokers & Dealers Ltd**
antation House
Mincing Lane
ndon EC3M 3DX
71) 626 9763

ank of England
readneedle Street
ndon EC2R 8AH
71) 601 4444

anking Ombudsman
itadel House
11 Fetter Lane
ndon EC4A 1BR
71) 583 1395

**lind Business
ssociation**
o 98 Aldborough Road
pminster
ssex RM14 2RS
4024) 58475
roup for the self-employed
ho are visually handicapped.

ritish Aerospace
1 Strand
ndon WC2N 5JT
71) 930 1020

**ritish Franchise
ssociation**
hames View
ewtown Road
enley-on-Thames
xon RG9 1HG
491) 578049
ade association for those
nnected with franchises.

**ritish Glass
anufacturers
onfederation**
orthumberland Road
heffield S10 2AU
742) 686201

**British Industry
Committee on South Africa**
45 Great Peter Street
London SW1P 3LT
(071) 222 5133

**British Insurance Brokers
Association (BIBA)**
14 Bevis Marks
London EC3A 7NT
(071) 623 9043

British Steel Corporation
9 Albert Embankment
London SE1 7SN
(071) 735 7654

**Business in the
Community**
227A City Road
London EC1V 1LX
(071) 253 3716
Promotion of involvement in the
local community by business.

British Shipbuilders
Clayton House
Regent Centre
Newcastle-upon-Tyne
NE3 3HW
(091) 213 0303

**Chatterley Whitfield
Mining Museum**
Nr Tunstall
Stoke-on-Trent ST6 8UN
(0782) 813337

**Chemical Industries
Association Ltd**
Kings Buildings
Smith Square
London SW1P 3JJ

Commercial Relations
States Office
Cyril Le Marquand House
The Parade
St. Helier
Jersey C.I.
(0534) 79111
Register of companies based in
Jersey. Search fee.

**Companies Registration
Office**
Companies House
55 City Road
London EC1
(071) 253 9393

**Confederation of British
Industry (CBI)**
Centre Point
103 New Oxford Street
London WC1A 1DU
(071) 379 7400

Dun & Bradstreet Ltd
Holmers Farm Way
High Wycombe
Bucks HP12 4UL
(0494) 422000
Business information services,
especially in the area of credit
ratings, both in the UK and
abroad. Also runs a marketing
operation and a debt collection
service.

**Engineering Industry
Training Board**
41 & 54 Clarendon Road
Watford
Herts WD1 1LB
(0923) 38441

**Equal Opportunities
Commission**
Overseas House
Quay Street
Manchester M3 3HN
(061) 833 9244

**Ethical Investment
Research Information
Service (EIRIS)**
9 Poland Street
London W1
(071) 439 2771
Provides a service for investors
who want to ensure that they
are not supporting a company
which operates in areas they
disapprove of, e.g. alcohol,
tobacco, etc.

European Investment Bank
68 Pall Mall
London SW1Y 5ES
(071) 839 3351

Fair Employment Commission
60 Great Victoria Street
Belfast BT2 7BB
(0232) 240020
Adjudicates on cases of discrimination on the grounds of religion or politics in Northern Ireland.

Financial Intermediaries, Managers and Brokers Regulatory Association (FIMBRA)
Hertsmere House
Hertsmere Road
London E14 4AB
(071) 538 8860/(071) 895 1229
Under the Financial Services Act 1986 anyone who carries on an investment business must be authorised to do so and FIMBRA regulates the firms who provide investment services and advice to the public.

French Chamber of Commerce
Knightsbridge House
197 Knightsbridge
London SW7 1RB
(071) 225 5250

Fullemploy Group Ltd
County House
190 Great Dover Street
London SE1 4YB
(071) 378 1774
Organisation aiming to improve employment prospects of the minority ethnic communities by offering training, economic support and advice.

General Registry, Deeds & Companies
Finch Road
Douglas
Isle of Man
(0624) 673358
Property and other legal records, also details of companies and business names, both live and inactive, registered in the Isle of Man.

Greater Manchester Museum of Science & Industry
Liverpool Road
Manchester M3 4JP
(061) 832 2244

Guild of Master Craftsmen
166 High Street
Lewes
Sussex BN7 1XU
(0273) 478449

Highlands & Islands Enterprise
Bridge House
20 Bridge Street
Inverness
Scotland IV1 1QR
(0463) 234171

Hotel & Catering Training Company
International House
High Street
London W5 5DB
(081) 579 2400

Indian Workers Association
112A The Green
Southall
Middlesex UB2 4BQ
(081) 574 7283

The Industrial Society
Quadrant Court
49 Calthorpe Road
Edgbaston
Birmingham B15 1TH
(021) 454 6769

Industrial Tribunals for England & Wales
93 Ebury Bridge Road
London SW1W 8RE
(071) 730 9161

Institute of Directors
116 Pall Mall
London SW1Y 5ED
(071) 839 1233

Institute for Fiscal Stud
7 Ridgmount Street
London WC1E 7AE
(071) 636 3784

Institute of Manpower Studies
Mantell Building
University of Sussex
Falmer
Brighton
East Sussex BN1 9RF
(0273) 686751
Research into employment labour markets, training, etc. Range of publications.

Institute of Personnel Management (IPM)
Camp Road
Wimbledon
London SW19 4UX
(081) 946 9100

Insurance Ombudsman Bureau
31 Southampton Row
London WC1B 5HJ
(071) 242 8613

The International Stock Exchange
Old Broad Street
London EC2N 1HP
(071) 588 2355

The Judicial Greffe
10 Hill Street
St Helier
Jersey C.I.
(0534) 75472

**hting Industry
deration**
an house
7 Balham Road
idon SW17 7BQ
1) 675 5432

yds of London
ime Street
idon EC3M 7DQ
1) 623 7100

**yds Register of
ipping**
Fenchurch Street
idon EC3M 4BS
1) 709 9166

idon Enterprise Agency
now Hill
idon EC1A 2BS
1) 236 3000
ately sponsored
anisation which helps in the
ablishment and running of
all businesses and promotes
er City regeneration.

**ttery Promotion
mpany**
Floral Street
idon WC2E 9DG
1) 836 7399

**il Order Traders'
sociation**
Castle Street
erpool L2 4TD
1) 236 7581

**e Market Research
ciety**
Northburgh Street
idon EC1V 0AH
1) 490 4911

**nopolies & Mergers
mmission**
w Court
Carey Street
idon WC2A 2JE
1) 831 6111

**Motor Industry Research
Unit Ltd (MIRU)**
2 Dove Street
Norwich NR2 1DE
(0603) 614991

**National Economic
Development Office
(NEDO)**
Millbank Tower
Millbank
London SW1P 4QX
(071) 217 4043
Forum for government,
management, trades union and
other interests to come together
and produce initiatives to
benefit British industry.

**National Federation of the
Self-Employed and Small
Businesses Ltd**
32 St Anne's Road West
Lytham St Annes
Lancashire FY8 1NY
(0253) 720911

**National Market Traders
Federation**
Hampton House
Hawshaw Lane
Hoyland
Barnsley
Yorks S74 0HA
(0226) 749021

**National Union of
Mineworkers (NUM)**
Holly Street
Sheffield S1 2GT
(0742) 766900

Northern Development Co
Bank House
Carliol Square
Newcastle upon Tyne
NE1 6XE
(091) 261 5131

**Northern Ireland
Economic Research
Centre**
48 University Road
Belfast BT7 1NJ
(0232) 325594

Office of Fair Trading
Field House
Bream's Buildings
London EC4A 1PR
(071) 242 2858

Patent Office
State House
66-71 High Holborn
London WC1R 4TP
(071) 831 2525

Sales Branch
Unit 6
9 Mile Point
Cross Keys
Newport
Gwent NP1 7HZ
(0495) 201100

**Pensions Management
Institute**
PMI House
124 Middlesex Street
London E1 7HY
(071) 247 1452

**The Prince's Youth
Business Trust**
8th Floor
Melbury House
Melbury Terrace
London NW1 6LZ
(071) 262 1340

REACH
83 Southwark Street
London SE1 0HD
(071) 928 0452
Agency placing retired
executives in part-time,
expenses-only work with
voluntary organisations.

**Registrar of Companies
for Scotland**
102 George Street
Edinburgh EH2 3DJ
(031) 225 5774

The Registrar-General
Greffe
St. Peter Port
Guernsey C.I.
(0481) 25277
Registry of business and all
court work.

Remploy Ltd
415 Edgware Road
London NW2 6LR
(081) 452 8020
Provides sheltered employment
for disabled people in many
different industries and trades
throughout the country.

**Royal National Institute
for the Blind Small
Business Unit**
224 Great Portland Street
London W1N 6AA
(071) 388 1266
Advice and help for visually
handicapped people who would
like to set up a business.

**Royal Society for the
Encouragement of Arts,
Manufacture & Commerce
(RSA)**
8 John Adam Street
London WC2N 6EZ
(071) 930 5115

**Rural Development
Commission**
141 Castle Stret
Salisbury
Wiltshire SP1 3TP
(0722) 336255
Business service for small firms.

11 Cowley Street
London SW1P 3NA
(071) 276 6969
Advises government on rural
affairs, gives advice, training
and loans to small businesses
in rural areas and supports
community projects.

**Scottish Development
Agency**
120 Bothwell Street
Glasgow G2 7JT
(041) 248 2700

**Scottish Trades Union
Congress**
16 Woodlands Terrace
Glasgow G3 6DF
(041) 332 4946

**Securities & Investments
Board**
Gavrelle House
2-14 Bunhill Row
London EC14 8RA
(071) 638 1240

Shaw Trust
Caithness House
Western Way
Melksham
Wiltshire SN12 8DZ
(0225) 790860
Identifies employment
opportunities in industry and
commerce for people with
severe disabilities.

Small Firms Service
Department of Employment
Steel House
Tothill Street
London SW1H 9NF
(071) 273 4728
Government service providing
information and advice to small
firms.

The Stock Exchange
Old Broad Street
London EC2N 1HP
(071) 588 2355

**Trades Union Congress
(TUC)**
Congress House
Great Russell Street
London WC1B 3LS
(071) 636 4030

Women & Manual Trades
52-54 Featherstone Street
London EC1Y 8RT
(071) 251 9192
Register of tradeswomen.

**Welsh Development
Agency**
Pearl House
Greyfriars Road
Cardiff
Wales CF1 3XX
(0222) 222666

Education

Addresses:
**Adult Literacy & Basic
Skills Unit (ALBSU)**
Kingsbourne House
High Holborn
London WC1V 7DA
(071) 405 4017
(England & Wales) Governme
funded body which advises,
sponsors development project
and training and publishes
publicity and tutors' material.

**Advisory Centre for
Education (ACE)**
Unit 1B
Aberdeen Studios
22-24 Highbury Grove
London N5 2EA
(071) 354 8318
Information about all aspects o
education.

**Association for the
Education and Welfare of
the Visually Handicapped**
c/o 24 Vicarage Road
Harborne
Birmingham B17 0SP
(021) 426 6815

**Association of Common-
wealth Universities**
John Foster House
36 Gordon Square
London WC1H 0PF
(071) 387 8572

**The Boarding Schools
Association**
Watendlath
Bug Hill
Warlingham
Surrey CR3 9LT
(0883) 624717

**British Dyslexia
Association**
98 London Road
Reading
Berks RG1 5AU
(0734) 668271/2

Campaign for the Advancement of State Education
25 Leybourne Park
Kew Gardens
Surrey TW9 3HT
(081) 940 4771

Central Bureau for Educational Visits & Exchanges (CBEVE)
Seymour Mews House
Seymour Mews
London W1H 9PE
(071) 486 5101
National office for information and advice on educational visits and exchanges. Produces publications on travelling, working and studying abroad.

Central Council for Education & Training in Social Work (CCETSW)
Derbyshire House
St. Chad's Street
London WC1H 8AD
(071) 278 2455

Committee of Directors of Polytechnics
Kirkman House
12-14 Whitfield Street
London W1P 6AX
(071) 636 0068

Committee of Vice-Chancellors and Principals of the Universities of the United Kingdom
29 Tavistock Square
London WC1H 9EZ
(071) 387 9231
Has a number of specialist sub-committees as well as running the Universities Information Unit, the central press office for UK universities.

Council for National Academic Awards (CNAA)
344-345 Gray's Inn Road
London WC1X 8PB
(071) 278 4411
Approves the award of degrees by polytechnics and colleges.

CUSS
32 Cowbridge Road East
Canton
Cardiff CF1 9DU
(0222) 226188
Organisation that works with people who have learning difficulties.

Education Otherwise
25 Common Lane
Hemingford Abbots
Cambridgeshire PE18 9AN
(0926) 886828
Information and advice about educating children at home.

The Engineering Council
10 Maltravers Street
London WC2R 3ER
(071) 240 7891
Supervises the engineering profession, sets standards for individual registration, accreditation for academic courses and practical training in industry. Runs WISE (Women Into Science & Engineering).

ESCAPE
Tregeraint House
Zennor
St Ives
Cornwall TR26 3DB
Association which helps teachers seeking a career change.

Grant-Maintained Schools Trust
239-245 Vauxhall Bridge Road
London SW1V 1EJ
(071) 828 9855

Housebound Learners
Horham School
Charlwood Road
London SW15
(081) 788 2157

Independent Schools Information Service (ISIS)
56 Buckingham Gate
London SW1E 6AG
(071) 630 8793/4

Muslim Educational Trust
130 Stroud Green Road
London N4 3RZ
(071) 272 8502

National Advisory Centre on Careers for Women
8 Artillery Row
London SW1P 1RT
(071) 799 2129

National Association for Gifted Children
Park Campus
Boughton Green Road
Northampton NN2 7AL
(0604) 792300

National Association for Remedial Education (NARE)
2 Lichfield Road
Stafford ST17 4JX
(0785) 46872

National Association of Governors & Managers (NAGM)
21 Bennets Hill
Birmingham B2 5QP
(021) 643 5787
Non-party association concerned with the involvement and training of school governors.

National Association of Head Teachers
1 Heath Square
Boltro Road
Haywards Heath
West Sussex RH16 1BL
(0444) 458133

National Confederation of Parent/Teacher Associations
2 Ebbs Fleet Industrial Estate
Stonebridge Road
Gravesend
Kent DA11 9DZ
(0474) 560618

National Council for Educational Technology
3 Devonshire Street
London W1N 2BA
(071) 636 4186
Government-aided organisation.

National Foundation for Educational Research
The Mere
Upton Park
Slough
Bucks SL1 2DQ
(0753) 74123

National Society for Education in Art & Design
7A High Street
Corsham
Wiltshire SN13 0ES
(0249) 714825

National Union of Students (NUS)
Nelson Mandela House
461 Holloway Road
London N7 6LJ
(071) 272 9445

National Union of Teachers
Hamilton House
Mabledon Place
London WC1H 9BD
(071) 388 6191

Open University
Walton Hall
Milton Keynes
Bucks MK7 6AA
(0908) 274066

School Examinations & Assessment Council (SEAC)
Newcombe House
45 Notting Hill Gate
London W11 3JB
(071) 229 1234
Government agency to review all aspects of school examinations, etc.

Scottish Community Education Council (SCEC)
West Coates House
90 Haymarket Terrace
Edinburgh EH12 5LQ
(031) 313 2488
Information and resource centre for informal education in community groups. Has a section for adult literacy and numeracy.

Scottish Parent Teacher Council
30 Rutland Square
Edinburgh EH1 2BW
(031) 228 4726

Standing Conference on Schools' Science and Technology
76 Portland Place
London W1N 4AA

University Funding Council
14 Park Crescent
London W1N 4DH
(071) 636 7799

Workers Education Association (WEA)
9 Upper Berkeley Street
London W1H 8BY
(071) 402 5608

The Environment

Publications:

CAB Abstracts (pub. CAB International, Wallingford, Oxon OX10 8DE, (0491) 32111
Bibliographic database of research on world agriculture forestry, soil, etc. Published in journal form or by on-line access. Fees on request.

The Green Consumer Guide (pub. Gollancz)
John Elkington & Julia Hailes
Looks at the environmental implications of high-street purchases and offers advice to consumers.

Red Data Book (pub. International Union for the Conservation of Nature & Natural Resources, Switzerland)
(2 books: one animals, other birds. Volumes on amphibians reptiles and plantlife planned)
Looseleaf reference book of endangered wildlife; their former and present distribution estimates of numbers remaining; breeding rate in the wild and captivity; why endangered and conservation measures being taken to protect them.

Addresses:

Action for Communities in Rural England (ACRE)
Stroud Road
Cirencester
Gloucestershire GL7 6JR
(0285) 653477

Ark Trust
498-500 Harrow Road
London W9 3QA
(081) 968 6780

**sociation for the
nservation of Energy**
herlock Mews
don W1M 3RH
1) 935 1495

**sociation of Facilities
nagers**
Derek Butcher
C Wood Lane
don W12 7RJ
1) 576 1858
ociation of those
ponsible for the design and
ishing of business premises
nsure the physical and
chological well-being of
kers.

**tish Ornithologists
ion**
British Museum (Natural
tory)
-Dept of Ornithology
ng
rts HP23 6AP
42) 890080
ociation for professional
thologists (not birdwatchers).

**e British Pest Control
sociation**
t James' Court
ar Gate
rby DE1 1ZU

**tish Trust for
nithology**
e Nunnery
nnery Place
etford
folk IP24 2PU
42) 750050

**ntre on Accessible
vironments**
Great Smith Street
don SW1P 3OJ
1) 222 7980
rmation and advisory
vice on environmental needs
isabled people.

Civic Trust
17 Carlton House Terrace
London SW1X 5AW
(071) 930 0914

**Council for the Protection
of Rural England (CPRE)**
Warwick House
25 Buckingham Palace
Road
London SW1W 0PP
(071) 235 9481

Countryside Commission
John Dower House
Crescent Place
Cheltenham
Gloucestershire GL50 3RA
(0242) 521381
Government's official advisor
on countryside matters.

Eco Surveys Ltd.
Station Street
Ruskington
Sleaford
Lincs NG34 9DG
(0526) 833794
Wildlife survey consultants,
working mainly on rivers, but
also on farms, ponds and lakes
to preserve flora and fauna.

**European Space Agency
(ESA)**
8-10 Rue Mario Nikis
75738 Paris
France
(010-33-1) 42 73 7654

Forestry Commission
231 Costorphine Road
Edinburgh EH12 7AT
(031) 334 0303

Freedom of Information
88 Old Street
London EC1V 9AR
(071) 253 2445

Friends of the Earth (FOE)
26-28 Underwood Street
London N1 7JQ
(071) 490 1555

Georgian Group
37 Spital Square
London E1 6DY
(071) 377 1722
Advisory group on listed
buildings.

Greenpeace
Canonbury Villas
London N1 2PN
(071) 354 5100
Campaigning ecology group in
the areas of wildlife, nuclear,
toxic and air pollution.

**Henry Doubleday
Research Association,
National Centre for
Organic Gardening**
Ryton-on-Dunsmore
Coventry CV8 3LG
(0203) 303517
Promotes organic principles in
gardening.

**Industry Council for
Packaging and the
Environment**
Premier House
10 Greycoat Place
London SW1P 1SB
(071) 222 8865

**Institute of Agricultural
History and Museum of
English Rural Life**
University of Reading
Whiteknights
P.O. Box 229
Reading
Berks RG6 2AG
(0734) 875123

**Institute of
Oceanographic Sciences**
Deacon Laboratories
Brook Road
Wormley
Godalming
Surrey GU8 5UB
(0428) 684141

Bidston Observatory
Birkenhead
Cheshire L43 7RA
(051) 653 8633

Research units of the National Environment Research Council (q.v.).

Institute of Terrestrial Ecology
Merlewood Research Station
Grange-over-Sands
Cumbria LA11 6JU
(05395) 32264

Institution of Environmental Health Officers
Chadwick House
Rushworth Street
London SE1 0QT
(071) 928 6006

International Maritime Organisation
4 Albert Embankment
London SE1 7SR
(071) 735 7611
United Nations agency responsible for maritime safety and the prevention of marine pollution.

International Waterfowl and Wetlands Research Bureau
Slimbridge
Gloucestershire GL2 7BX
(0453) 890624

Marine Conservation Society
4 Gloucester Road
Ross-on-Wye
Hereford HR9 5BU
(0989) 66017

Marine Education and Research Ltd
17 Hartington Park
Bristol BS6 7ES
(0272) 249109

Meteorological Office
London Road
Bracknell
Berks RG12 2SZ
(0344) 420242

National Society for Clean Air
136 North Street
Brighton BN1 1RG
(0273) 26313
Campaign against air pollution of all kinds, lead in petrol, acid rain, industrial pollution, noise, etc.

The National Trust
36 Queen Anne's Gate
London SW1H 9AS
(071) 222 9251

National Trust for Scotland
5 Charlotte Square
Edinburgh EH2 4DU
(031) 226 5922

Nature Conservancy Council
Northminster House
Northminster Road
Peterborough PE1 1UA
(0733) 340345

Noise Abatement Society
P.O. Box 8
Bromley
Kent BR2 0UH
(081) 460 3146

North Wales Wildlife Trust
376 High Street
Bangor ·
Gwynedd LL57 1YE
(0248) 351541

Parents Against Tobacco
46 Arundel Street
Brighton BN2 5TH
(0273) 601312

The Ramblers Association
1-5 Wandsworth Road
London SW8 2XX
(071) 582 6878

Royal Botanical Gardens
Kew
Richmond
Surrey TW9 3AB
(081) 940 1171

Royal Greenwich Observatory
Maddingley Road
Cambridge
Cambs CB3 0AZ
(0223) 374000

Royal Society for Nature Conservation
The Green
Witham Park
Waterside South
Nettleham
Lincoln LN5 7JR
(0522) 544400

Royal Society for the Protection of Birds
The Lodge
Sandy
Beds SG19 2DL
(0767) 680551

The Scott Polar Research Institute
Lensfield Road
Cambridge CB2 1ER
(0223) 336540
Current scientific work on the Arctic and Antarctic, also expedition relics, Eskimo and general polar art.

Soil Association
86 Colston Street
Bristol BS1 5BB
(0272) 290661

Tidy Britain Group
The Pier
Wigan
Lancs WM3 4EX
(0942) 824620

Tornado & Storm Research Organisation
54 Frome Road
Bradford-on-Avon
Wiltshire BA15 1LD
(02216) 2482

UK Cycle Campaign Network/ London Cycle Campaign
3 Stamford Street
London SE1 9NT
(071) 928 7220

⊓ited Kingdom Nirex Ltd
⎺rie Avenue
⎺rwell
⎺dcot
⎺on OX11 0RH
⎺35) 833009
⎺-ordinates proposals for the
⎺nagement and disposal of
⎺io-active waste.

⎺ater Research Centre
⎺O. Box 16
⎺nley Road
⎺dmenham
⎺arlow
⎺cks SL7 2HD
⎺491) 571531

⎺omen's Environmental
⎺twork
⎺7 City Road
⎺ndon EC1V 1LA
⎺71) 354 8823

⎺e Woodland Trust
⎺tumn Park
⎺antham
⎺ncs NG31 6LL
⎺arity concerned with
⎺eserving Britain's native
⎺odlands.

⎺orld Conservation
⎺onitoring Centre
⎺9c Huntingdon Road
⎺ambridge CB3 0DL
⎺223) 277314

⎺RC
⎺O. Box 16
⎺arlow
⎺cks SL7 2HD
⎺491) 571531
⎺dependent, research-based
⎺mpany which looks into water
⎺dustry problems worldwide.

⎺ological Society of
⎺ndon
⎺egent's Park
⎺ndon NW1 4RY
⎺71) 722 3333

Facts

Publications:
The Annual Register (pub. Longmans)
Record of world events: political, scientific, legal, cultural, economic and sporting.

*Aslib Directory of Information Sources in the UK (pub. Aslib) Ed. Ellen M. Codlin : Vol 1: Science Technology & Commerce;
Vol 2: Social Sciences, Medicine & the Humanities.
Lists libraries, associations and learned societies.

Chambers Dictionary of Dates (pub. Chambers 1983)

Encyclopaedia of Dates & Events (ed. L.C. Pascoe, pub. Hodder 1979)

English Historical Documents (pub. Eyre Methuen).
12 volumes covering the period 500AD-1914AD; texts of all kinds of documents from private diaries to Acts of Parliament.

General Household Survey/Family Expenditure Survey/Labour Force Survey/International Passenger Survey, etc.
Statistical information compiled by the Office of Population Censuses & Surveys (pub. HMSO).

Hollis Press & Public Relations Annual (pub. annually, Hollis Directories Ltd, Contact House, Sunbury-on-Thames, Middx TW16 5HG (0932) 784781).

Directory of news contacts in commerce, industry, consumer affairs, sports, finance, etc. Sections on sponsorship, public relations, voluntary bodies.

Index to Theses accepted for Higher Degrees in the Universities of Great Britain & Ireland (pub. Aslib)
N.B. Oxford, Cambridge and London Universities publish separate annual lists.

Janes Publishing Co. Ltd.
238 City Road
London EC1V 2PU
(081) 883 1831/2201
Publish an exhaustive series of reference books on trains and boats and planes, both civil and military, with technological information and names of manufacturers.

*Keesings Record of World Events (formerly Keesing's Contemporary Archives, pub. Longmans).

Lloyd's Register of Shipping
Technical information and owners of 76,000 ships. Updated monthly from computer base.

Notes & Queries (pub. quarterly Oxford University Press).
Describes itself as being about English language and literature; but is, especially the earlier volumes, an eclectic ragbag of information linguistic, biographical and historical. The British Library has a complete set, which is indexed, on the open shelves. Worth consulting for the kind of fact that you never realised you wanted to know.

Webster's Biographical Dictionary

*Willings Press Guide
(pub. annually British Media
Publications, Windsor
Court, East Grinstead
House, East Grinstead,
West Sussex RH19 1XA
(0342) 36972)
List of all newspapers,
magazines and journals
published in the UK, also many
published abroad.

Addresses:
**Association of
Independent Museums**
Weald & Downland Open
Air Museum
Singleton
Sussex PO18 0EU
(024363) 348

**Association of Special
Libraries & Information
Bureaux (Aslib)**
20-24 Old Street
London EC1V 9AP
(071) 253 4488

BBC Data Enquiry Service
Room 7
1 Portland Place
London W1A 1AA
(071) 927 5998
Access to BBC's information
resources: press cuttings and
reference libraries; indexes to
BBC radio and television output
and to news bulletins;
pronunciation unit and negative
checks. Also accesses other
commercial databases, e.g.
Nexis, Dialog. Fees on request.

**BBC Transcripts & Tapes
Unit**
c/o Secretariat
Broadcasting House
London W1A 1AA
(071) 927 5777
Non-broadcasting, non-
commercial requests for radio,
TV scripts, recordings of radio
programmes and material from
Sound Archives. Fees on
request.

**BBC Written Archives
Centre**
Caversham Park
Reading
Berks RG4 8TZ
(0734) 472742
Written material from 1922 to
1960s, not film or sound tapes.

Bodleian Library
Broad Street
Oxford OX1 3BG
(0865) 277000

Book Data
Northumberland House
2 King Street
Twickenham
Middx TW1 3RZ
(081) 892 2272
Company which offers
information about publications,
e.g. those on a particular
subject, from participating
publishers. Good on recent
publications. Fees on request.

British Library
British Museum
Great Russell Street
London WC1B 3DG
(071) 636 1544
A reader's ticket is necessary to
use the various reading rooms;
a 2-week ticket can be issued
on proof of identity (passport,
driver's licence or similar) to
use material not available at
another library. For longer term
tickets, a letter of reference
from the organisation wanting
the research or a detailed letter
stating the type of research to
be done is necessary.

**British Library
(Newspapers)**
Colindale Avenue
London NW9 5HE
(081) 200 5515
The main repository for British
newspapers and magazines
(some are kept at the British
Museum Reading Room). Also
has a large collection of
overseas publications.

Catholic Central Library
47 Francis Street
London SW1P 1DN
(071) 834 6128

**Central Office of
Information**
Hercules Road
London SE1 7DU
(071) 928 2345

**Centre for South Asian
Studies**
Laundress Lane
Cambridge CB2 1SD
(0223) 338094
Specialist library, also has
archives of private papers from
the Raj, missionaries, etc.

**Costume & Fashion
Research Centre**
4 Circus
Bath BA1 2EW
(0225) 461111 Ext. 2751
Attached to the Museum of
Costume, one of the largest
and most comprehensive
collections in the world.

Dr Williams Library
14 Gordon Square
London WC1H 0AG
(071) 387 3727
Non-conformist historical
material, general theology and
philosophy.

Fawcett Library
Calcutta House
Old Castle Street
London E1 7NT
(071) 283 1030
Britain's main specialist library
on women: both historical and
contemporary.

**Foreign & Commonwealth
Office Library**
Cornwall House
Stamford Street
London SE1 9NS
(071) 217 2007/8
Public reading room contains
complete Commonwealth
legislation. Also wide collection

95

ADDRESSES & REFERENCE BOOKS

istorical books on all foreign
intries (except India) and
ge collection of 19th century
onial photographs

ildhall Library
lermanbury
ndon EC2P 2EJ
71) 606 3030
cord office for the City of
idon.

perial War Museum
mbeth Road
ndon SE1 6HZ
71) 735 8922

dia Office Library
7 Blackfriars Road
ndon SE1 8NG
71) 928 9531

**stitute of Historical
esearch**
nate house
alet Street
ndon WC1E 7HU
71) 636 0272

orary of Congress
mes Madison Building
dependence Avenue S.E.
540 Washington D.C.
S.A.
10-1-202) 707 5000
nerican equivalent of the
tish Library.

arx Memorial Library
a Clerkenwell Green
ndon EC1R 0DU
71) 253 1485
story of socialism and
mmunism in Britain and
road. Collections on
nartism and early radical
ovements; the International
gade Archives from the
anish Civil War and the
nerican Labour Movement.

**ead Data Central
ternational**
ernational House
St. Katherine's Way
ndon E1 9UN
71) 488 9187

American-based company
which holds a number of
computer files accessing
information from publications in
the fields of news, medicine,
law, politics, accounting,
advertising and P.R. both in
Europe and the U.S. Fees on
request.

Methodist Archives
The John Rylands
University Library of
Manchester
Deansgate
Manchester M13 3EH
(061) 834 5343

Museums Association
34 Bloomsbury Way
London WC1A 2SF
(071) 404 4767
The Museums Association
publishes *Museums UK*, a
computer database covering
information about 1,750
museums and art galleries
(there are about 2,200 in
Britain) in this country. Statistics
included cover everything from
finance to conservation policy.
Also publishes a yearbook.

National Army Museum
Royal Hospital Road
London SW3 4HT
(071) 730 0717

National Library of Ireland
Kildare Street
Dublin 2
(0001) 618811

**National Library of
Scotland**
George IV Bridge
Edinburgh EH1 1EW
(031) 226 4531

National Library of Wales
Aberystwyth
Dyfed SY23 3BU
(0970) 623816

National Maritime Museum
Greenwich
London SE10 9NF
(081) 858 4422

**National Museums of
Scotland**
Chambers Street
Edinburgh EH1 1JF
(031) 225 7534

**Office of Population
Censuses & Surveys**
10 Kingsway
London WC2B 6JP
(071) 242 0262

Pattern Room
Ministry of Defence
c/o Royal Ordinance plc
Kings Meadow Road
Nottingham NG2 1EQ
(0602) 352028
Contains the world's largest
collection of modern small arms
(i.e. up to 40mm calibre).
About 50% of the holdings are
British.

Polish Library
238-246 King Street
London W6 0RF
(081) 741 0474
Books on Polish matters,
including underground
publications. Also has a
collection of photographs.

Priaulx Library
Candie Road
St. Peter Port
Guernsey C.I.
(0481) 721998
Local history, also holds
censuses, parish registers and
local newspapers on microfilm.

Public Record Office
Four Courts
Dublin 7
(010 3531) 725555

Public Record Office of Northern Ireland
66 Balmoral Avenue
Belfast BT9 6NY
(0232) 661621
Archives and records of government departments and non-departmental public bodies together with a wide range of private records, including those of the church. Established 1923 so many records complete only from that date.

Public Records Office
(Modern Departmental Records)
Ruskin Avenue
Kew
Richmond
Surrey TW9 4DU
(Medieval, Early Modern and Legal Records and the Census Returns)
Chancery Lane
London WC2A 1LR
(081) 876 3444
Vast archive of records of all kinds — there is a published guide to them which details holdings available at the PRO.

RAF Museums
Hendon
London NW9 5LL
(081) 205 2266
Aviation history, Battle of Britain Museum and Bomber Command Museum.

Rhodes House Library
South Parks Road
Oxford OX1 3RG
(0865) 270909
Specialist library on non-India, Commonwealth and the USA.

Royal Commission on Historical Manuscripts/ National Register of Archives
Quality House
Quality Court
Chancery Lane
London WC2A 1HP
(071) 242 1198

University of London Library
Senate House
Malet Street
London WC1E 7HU
(071) 636 4514
Open to non-members at the discretion of the Director. Holds, in addition to the general collection of books, a number of specialised bibliographies in many subjects and special collections of books. Also has a list of Ph.D. theses in progress.

The Weiner Library
4 Devonshire Street
London W1N 2BH
(071) 636 7247
Primarily material on the Holocaust but also has German history, Jewish history and contemporary history in the Middle East.

Wellcome Institute for the History of Medicine Library
The Wellcome Building
160 Euston Road
London NW1 2BP
(071) 387 4477

The Family & Social Welfare

Publications:
Charities Digest (pub. annually by the Family Welfare Association
501-503 Kingsland Road
London E8 4AU
(071) 254 6251)
Classified digest of charities with the services they offer an qualifications for receiving he where applicable.

The Voluntary Agencies Directory (pub. National Council of Voluntary Organisations
26 Bedford Square
London WC1B 3HU)

Addresses:
Action for Benefits
c/o NUSCPS
124-130 Southwark Street
London SE1 0TU
(071) 928 9671
Campaigning group for improved welfare benefit system both for administrative staff and recipients.

Action on Addiction
York House
199 Westminster Bridge Road
London SE1 0TU
(071) 928 9671

Age Concern England
Astral House
1268 London Road
London SW16 4ER
(081) 679 8000

lcoholics Anonymous
(General Service Office)
O. Box 1
onebow House
onebow
ork YO1 2NJ
904) 644026

sian Family Counselling
ervice
quity Chambers
Piccadilly
adford BD1 3NN
274) 720486

The Avenue
ndon W13 8LB
81) 997 5749
ounselling and advice service
milar to RELATE for Asian
milies.

ssistance Dogs for
isabled People
Slipper Road
msworth
ampshire PO10 8BS
243) 375723
harity aiming to supply
verely disabled people with
gs trained to do many
eryday tasks.

ssociation for Sexual
nd Marital Therapists
.O. Box 62
heffield S10 3TS

ssociation of Blind
sians
Stranraer Way
eeling Street
ff Caledonian Road
ndon N1 ODR
71) 609 3590

he Association for
ost-Natal Illness
Gowan Avenue
ndon SW6 6RH
71) 731 4867

he Birmingham
ettlement
8 Summer Lane
rmingham B19 3LR
21) 359 3562

Major debt-counselling
organisation. Special helpline
for housing debt.

British Agencies for
Adoption & Fostering
11 Southwark Street
London SE1 1RQ
(071) 407 8800

British Association for
Counselling
1 Regent Place
Rugby CV21 2PJ
(0788) 578328
Information about various types
of counselling and psychotherapy.

British Association of
Social Workers
16 Kent Street
Birmingham B5 6RD
(021) 622 3911

British Institute of Funeral
Directors
11 Regent Street
Kingswood
Bristol BS15 2JX
(0272) 673609

British Limbless
Ex-Service Men's
Association
Frankland Moore House
185-187 High Road
Chadwell Heath
Romford
Essex RM6 6NA
(071) 590 1124/5

British Psychological
Society
St Andrews House
48 Princess Road East
Leicester LE1 7DR
(0535) 549568

British Refugee Council
Bondway House
3 Bondway
London SW8 1SJ
(071) 582 6922

British Youth Council
57 Charlton Street
London NW1 1HU
(071) 387 7559/5882

Campaign for
Homosexual Equality
(CHE)
38 Mount Pleasant
London WC1X 0AP
(071) 833 3912

Carers' National
Association
29 Chilworth Mews
London W2 3RG
(071) 724 7776

Catholic Marriage
Advisory Council
Clitheroe House
1 Blythe Mews
Blythe Road
London W14 0NW
(071) 371 1341

Centre for Policy on
Ageing
25-31 Ironmonger Row
London EC1V 3QP
(071) 253 1787

Centre on Environment
for the Handicapped (CEH)
35 Great Smith Street
London SW1P 3BJ
(071) 222 7980
Voluntary organisation
concerned with improving
building design to
accommodate the needs of all
users, including the elderly and
disabled.

Charities Information
Bureau
138 Digbeth
Birmingham B5 6DR
(021) 643 8477
Advice to voluntary groups on
sources of funding particularly
charity trusts covering mainly
West Midlands.

Charity Commission
St Albans House
57-60 Haymarket
London SW1Y 4QX
(071) 210 3000

Child Poverty Action Group
1-5 Bath Street
London EC1V 9PY
(071) 253 3406
Advice on welfare and social security benefits.

Childhope UK
25 Castlereagh Street
London W1H 5YR
(071) 402 4600
British branch of the International Movement on behalf of Streetchildren.

Child Line
50 Studd Street
London N1 0QD
(071) 239 1000
National helpline for children or young people in trouble or danger.

Children's Legal Centre
20 Compton Terrace
London N1 2UN
(071) 359 6251/2

Commission for Racial Equality
Elliot House
Allington Street
London SW1E 5EH
(071) 828 7022

Community Development Foundation
60 Highbury Grove
London N5 2AG
(071) 226 5375

Community Service Volunteers
237 Pentonville Road
London N1 9NJ
(071) 278 6601
Recruits and places young people to work as volunteers on a range of community projects:

radio and TV scheme; young offenders scheme.

Compassionate Friends
6 Denmark Street
Bristol BS1 5DQ
(0272) 292778
Support group for parents whose children have died.

Contact A Family
16 Strutton Ground
London SW1P 2HP
(071) 222 2695
Organisation which puts the parents of handicapped children in touch with each other. Also advises on benefits, specialist treatment, education, etc.

Counsel and Care for the Elderly
16 Bonny Street
London NW1 9LR
(071) 485 1550

CRUSE
Cruse House
126 Sheen Road
Richmond
Surrey TW9 1UR
(081) 940 4818/9047
Bereavement counselling.

Crysis Support Group
BM Crysis
London WC1N 3XX
(071) 404 5011
Help and advice for parents with a crying baby.

Disability Alliance ERA
Universal House
88-94 Wentworth Street
London E1 7SA
(071) 247 8776
Financial advice service for people with disabiities. Also campaigns for the introduction of a comprehensive disability income scheme.

Disability Benefits Consortium
4 Wilkinson House
Cherbury Street
London N1 6TH
(071) 739 0810
Campaigns for a comprehensive disability allowance.

Disabled Living Foundation
380-384 Harrow Road
London W9 2HU
(071) 289 6111
Centre with wide variety of aid and equipment for the disable

The Disablement Income Group (DIG)
Millmead Business Centre
Millmead Road
London N17 9QU
(081) 801 8013

DIG Scotland
ECAS House
28-30 Howden Street
Edinburgh EH8 9HW
(031) 667 0249

Eating Disorders Association
(0494) 521431

English Collective of Prostitutes
King's Cross Women's Centre
71 Tonbridge Street
London WC1H 9DZ
(071) 837 7509

EPOCH
77 Holloway Road
London N7 8JZ
(071) 700 0627

Families Need Fathers
BM Families
London WC1N 3XX
(081) 886 0970

upport and campaigning
oup for changes in family law
ensure that in cases of
rental separation children
aintain contact with both
rents.

amily Rights Group
9 Manor Gardens
olloway Road
ondon N7 6LA
71) 263 9724
roup of social workers,
wyers and others concerned
th the legal aspects of
provement of practice
lating to children in care.

**amily Welfare
ssociation**
01-505 Kingsland Road
alston
ondon E8 4AU
71) 254 6251
harity founded to help
dividuals, families and groups
thin the community.

amblers Anonymous
7 Blantyre Street
ondon SW10 0DT
71) 352 3060
elf-help group for gamblers.

**eneral Council for
ducation & Training in
ocial Work (GCETSW)**
erbyshire House
t. Chad's Street
ondon WC1H 8AD
71) 278 2455

ingerbread
5 Wellington Street
ondon WC2E 7BN
71) 240 0953
dvice for single parents on
nance, the law and social
roblems. Local groups all over
e country.

**Guide Dogs for the Blind
Association**
Alexandra House
9-11 Park Street
Windsor
Berks SL4 1JR
(0753) 855711

Hearing Dogs for the Deaf
Training Centre
London Road (A40)
Lewknor
Oxon OX9 5RY
(0844) 53898

Help the Aged
16/18 St. James' Walk
London EC1R OBE
(071) 253 0253
Campaigning and fund-raising
organisation. Also provides
grants for various projects and
help with housing for the elderly.

Holiday Care Service
2 Old Bank Chambers
Station Road
Horley
Surrey RH6 9HW
(0293) 774535
Organisation which provides
information on holidays for
disabled people.

Holiday Helpers
P.O. Box 20
Horley
Surrey RH6 9UY
(0293) 775137
Project to enable disabled and
elderly people to take
independent holidays with the
help of suitably experienced
volunteers.

Incest Crisis Line
P.O. Box 32
Northolt
Middlesex UB5 4JG
(081) 890 4732

Independent Living Fund
Room 520
New Court
Carey Street
London WC2A 2LS

Charitable trust which gives
grants and one-off payments to
severely disabled people to
help them live independently in
their own homes.

**International Planned
Parenthood Federation
(IPPF)**
Regent's College
Inner Circle
London NW1 4NS
(071) 486 0741

Institute of Race Relations
2-6 Leeke Street
London WC1X 9HS
(071) 837 0041

Jewish Marriage Council
23 Ravenshurst Avenue
London NW4 4EL
(081) 203 6311

**Joint Council for the
Welfare of Immigrants
(JCWI)**
115 Old Street
London EC1V 9JR
(071) 251 8706

Kids Club Network
(formerly **The National Out
of School Alliance**)
279-281 Whitechapel Road
London E1 1BY
(071) 247 3009

Multiple Births Foundation
Institute of Obstetrics and
Gynaecology Trust
Queen Charlotte's &
Chelsea Hospital
Goldhawk Road
London W6 0XG
(081) 743 4666 Ext. 5201
Organisation offering support
and advice to parents of twins,
triplets or more. Also carries
out research into multiple births.

Narcotics Anonymous
P.O. Box 417
London SW10 0RS
(071) 351 6794
Self-help group for drug addicts.

National Association for the Childless (NAC)
318 Summer Lane
Birmingham B19 3RL
(021) 359 4887

National Association for Maternal & Child Welfare
Strode House
46-48 Osnaburgh Street
London NW1 3ND
(071) 383 4541
Promotes education of mothers and young children and professionals involved in childcare.

National Association of Bereavement Services
68 Charlton Street
Londond NW1 1JR

National Association of Funeral Directors
618 Warwick Road
Solihull
West Midlands B91 1AA
(021) 711 1343

National Association of Stammerers
Unit 309
156 Blackfriars Road
London SE1 8EN
(071) 721 7166

National Association of Volunteer Bureaux
St. Peter's College
College Road
Saltley
Birmingham B8 3TE
(021) 327 0265

National Association of Widows
54-57 Allison Street
Digbeth
Birmingham B5 5TH
(021) 643 8348

National Childbirth Trust
Alexandra House
Oldham Terrace
London W3 6NH
(081) 992 8637

National Childcare Campaign
Wesley House
4 Wild Court
London WC2B 5AU
(071) 405 5617
Co-ordinates local childcare campaigns to promote childcare provision for the under-fives.

National Childminding Association (NCMA)
8 Masons Hill
Bromley
Kent BR2 9EY
(081) 464 6164

National Children's Bureau
8 Wakley Street
London EC1V 7QE
(071) 278 9441
Concerned with the general well-being of children. Comprehensive library and information service covering all aspects of childhood; health,education,adoption, legal rights, drug abuse etc.

National Council for One Parent Families
255 Kentish Town Road
London NW5 2LX
(071) 267 1361

National Council for Voluntary Organisations (NCVO)
26 Bedford Square
London WC1B 3HU
(071) 636 4066
Co-ordinates voluntary organisations. Has a reference library.

National Family Conciliation Council
Shaftesbury Centre
Rodbourne
Swindon
Wilts SN2 2AV
(0793) 514055
Helps divorcing couples come to amicable agreements.

National Federation of Blind
Unity House
Smyth Street
Westgate
Wakefield
West Yorkshire WF1 1E
(0924) 291313

National Federation of Women's Institutes
104 New Kings Road
Fulham
London SW6 4LY
(071) 371 9300

National Gypsy Counc
Greengate Street
Oldham OL4 1DQ
(061) 665 1924

National Institute for Social Work
5-7 Tavistock Place
London WC1H 9SS
(071) 387 9681

National Organisation Work with Girls and Young Women
c/o The Pankhurst Centr
60-62 Nelson Street
Chorlton-on-Medlock
Manchester M13 9WP
(061) 274 3421
Association for those involv in work with young women; youth workers, social and community workers, and educators.

National Society for the Prevention of Cruelty t Children (NSPCC)
67 Saffron Hill
London EC1N 8RS
(071) 242 1626

National Union of Townswomen's Guilds
Chamber of Commerce House
75 Harbourne Road
Birmingham B15 3DA
(021) 456 3435

ational Youth
ureau/National
ssociation of Young
eople's Counselling &
dvisory Centres
7-23 Albion Street
eicester LE1 2GD
0533) 558763

ORCAP
New High Street
eadington
xford OX3 5AJ
0865) 750554

orthern Ireland
ssociation for
ounselling
ryson House
8 Bedford Street
elfast BT2 7FE
0232) 325835

orthern Ireland
ssociation for Mental
ealth
eacon House
4 University Street
elfast BT7 1HE
0232) 328474

orthern Ireland Council
r Voluntary Action
NICVA)
Annadale Avenue
elfast BT9 5FN
0232) 640011

orthern Ireland Council
n Alcoholism
Elmwood Avenue
elfast BT9 6AZ
232) 266 4434

utset Ltd
rake House
3 Creekside
ondon SE8 3DZ
81) 692 7141
harity committed to creating
aining and employment
portunities for the disabled.

**Parent to Parent
Information Adoption
Society (PPIAS)**
Lower Boddington
Daventry
Northants NN11 6YB

Parentline OPUS
106 Godstone Road
Whyteleafe
Surrey CR3 O6B
(081) 645 0469
Organisation for parents under
stress.

**Parents Against Injustice
(PAIN)**
2 Pledgdon Green
Nr Henham
Bishops Stortford
Herts CM22 6BH
(0279) 850545/850194
Support group for parents
wrongly accused of abusing/
neglecting their children.

Partially Sighted Society
Queens Road
Doncaster DN1 2NX
(0302) 323132

People First
Oxford House
Derbyshire Street
London E2 6HG
(071) 739 3890
Pressure group run by people
with learning difficulties and
other disabilities to campaign
for the rights of disabled people.

**Play Matters/National Toy
Libraries Association**
68 Churchway
London NW1 1LT
(071) 387 9592
National body for over 1,200 toy
libraries for children especially
the disabled.

Population Studies
LSE
Houghton Street
London WC2A 2AE
(071) 405 7686

Independent group carrying out
demographic studies.

The Post-Adoption Centre
Interchange Building
15 Wilkin Street
London NW5 3NG
(071) 284 0555

**Pre-School Playgroups
Association (PPA)**
61-63 Kings Cross Road
London WC1X 9LL
(071) 833 0991

**Racial Attacks Monitoring
Project (RAMP)**
6 Seymour Street
Highfields
Leicester LE2 OLB
(0533) 532928
Support and advice for black
people who have experienced
racial harassment or attacks.

Relate (formerly **The
Marriage Guidance
Council)**
Herbert Gray College
Little Church Street
Rugby CV21 3AP
(0788) 573241

Release
388 Old Street
London EC1V 9LT
(071) 729 9904
National drugs and legal advice
agency.

**REMAP/Royal Association
for Disability &
Rehabilitation**
Hazeldean
Ightham
Sevenoaks
Kent TN5 9AD
(0732) 883818
Central reference point for
groups of volunteer engineers
and remedial therapists all over
the country who design
supply, adapt and modify
appliances for the disabled to
suit individual needs.

Runnymede Trust
11 Princelet Street
London E1 6QH
(071) 375 1496
Research and information
organisation dealing with
immigrants, British-born black
people and race relations. Not
an advice service.

The Samaritans
17 Uxbridge Road
Slough
Bucks SL1 1SN
(0753) 32713

**Scottish Association for
Counselling**
c/o Queen Margaret's
College
Clerwood Terrace
Edinburgh EH12 8TS
(031) 339 8111 Ext. 253

**Scottish Association for
Mental Health**
Atlantic House
38 Gardiners Crescent
Edinburgh EH3 8DQ
(031) 229 9687

**Scottish Council on
Alcoholism**
147 Blythswood Street
Glasgow G2 4EN
(041) 333 9677

Sigma
BM Sigma
London WC1N 3XX
(071) 837 7324
Self-help society for the
partners of bi-sexual people in
marriage.

**Society for the Protection
of Unborn Children (SPUC)**
7 Tufton Street
London SW1P 3QN
(071) 222 5845

**Soldiers, Sailors,
Airmen's Families
Association (SSAFA)**
19 Queen Elizabeth Street
London SE1 2LP
(071) 403 8783

Welfare organisation for service
and ex-service families.

St Dunstan's
P.O. Box 4XB
12-14 Harcourt Street
London W1A 4XB
(071) 723 5021
Charity to help war-blinded men
and women.

**Standing Conference on
Drug Abuse (SCODA)**
1-4 Hatton Place
Hatton Garden
London EC1N 8ND
(071) 430 2341

Suzy Lamplugh Trust
14 East Sheen Avenue
London SW14 8AS
(081) 392 1839
Association for research into
aspects of missing persons and
support for family and friends of
those who have disappeared.

**Talking Newspapers for
the Blind**
90A High Street
Heathfield
East Sussex TN21 8JD
(0435) 866102

The Tavistock Centre
120 Belsize Lane
London NW3 5BA
(071) 435 7111
Outpatients clinic and training
centre working in the area of
psychotherapy for adolescents,
children and families. Has an
important library with computer
links to the USA and Europe.

Turning Point
New Loom House
101 Back Church Lane
London E1 1LU
(071) 702 2300
National voluntary agency for
rehabilitation, counselling and
care in the fields of drug and
alcohol abuse and mental
health.

**Visually Handicapped
Persons Computer Users
Group (VIPCUG)**
The Manor House
Fleckney
Leicester LE8 0AP
(0533) 403147

**Welsh Regional
Representative for
Alcohol Concern**
Eryl Wen
Eryl Place
Llandudno
(0492) 76841

**Women's Aid Federation
of England Ltd**
P.O. Box 391
Bristol BS99 7WS
(0272) 633494
London Office
(071) 251 6537
Refuges for women and
children.

**Working Mothers
Association**
77 Holloway Road
London N7 8JZ
(071) 700 5771/2

**WRVS (Women's Royal
Voluntary Service)**
234-244 Stockwell Road
London SW9 9SP
(071) 416 0146

Food, Drink & Other Consumer Affairs

Publications:

Consumer Congress Directory (pub. The Consumers' Association) comprehensive list of consumer associations.

Addresses:

Agricultural & Food Research Council
Polaris House
North Star Avenue
Swindon
(0793) 413200

Association of British Production Agencies
5 Abingdon Road
London W8 6AF
(071) 938 1011

Association of British Travel Agents (ABTA)
5 Newman Street
London W1P 4AH
(071) 637 2444

The Brewers Society
2 Portman Square
London W1H 0BB
(071) 486 4831

The Brewing Research Foundation
Nuttel Hall
Nutfield
Redhill
Surrey RH1 4HY
(0737) 822272

British Clothing Industry Association/British Fashion Council
7 Swallow Place
London W1R 7AA
(071) 408 0020

British Organic Farmers
86 Colston Street
Bristol BS1 5BB
(0272) 299666

British Standards Institution (BSI)
2 Park Street
London W1A 2BS
(071) 629 9000

Campaign for Real Ale (CAMRA)
34 Alma Road
St Albans
Herts AL1 3BW
(0727) 867201

Compassion in World Farming
20 Lavant Street
Petersfield
Hants GU32 3EW
(0730) 64208

Consumers' Association
2 Marylebone Road
London NW1 4DX
(071) 486 5544
Publishers of *Which?* and other consumer publications.

Council of Justice to Animals & Humane Slaughter Association
34 Blanche Lane
South Mimms
Potters Bar
Herts EN6 3PA
(0707) 59040

Flour Milling and Baking Research Organisation (FMBRA)
Chorleywood
Hertfordshire WD3 5SH
(0927) 84111

Food from Britain
301-344 Market Towers
New Covent Garden Market
London SW8 5NQ
(071) 720 2144

General Consumer Council for Northern Ireland
116 Holywood Road
Belfast BT4 1NY
(0232) 672488

Harveys Wine Museum
12 Denmark Street
Bristol BS1 5DQ
(0272) 277661
Unique collection of items connected with the production and enjoyment of wine. Extensive library.

Institute of Food Science and Technology
5 Cambridge Court
210 Shepherd's Bush Road
London W6 7NL
(071) 603 6316

International Wine & Food Society
108 Old Brompton Road
London SW7 3RA
(071) 370 0909

Local Authorities Co-Ordinating Body on Trading Standards
P.O. Box 6
Token House
1A Robert Street
Croydon CR9 1LG
(081) 688 1996
Advisory body for local councils in the area of trading standards, weights and measures, food composition and quality legislation.

Mail Order Trader's Association (MOTA)
25 Castle Street
Liverpool L2 4TD
(051) 236 7581

Museum of Cider
Pomona Place
Off Whitecross Road
Hereford HR4 0LW
(0432) 354207
Traditional farm cider-making and growth of modern factory methods.

National Agriculture Centre
Stoneleigh
Warwickshire CV8 2RX
Enquiries; (0203) 696969
Houses a variety of associations connected with agriculture including cattle and rare breeds societies, goat and beekeeping groups, rural crafts, etc.

National Consumer Council
20 Grosvenor Gardens
London SW1W 0DH
(071) 730 3469
Money Advice Association at same address gives free confidential advice to people with money problems.

National Farmers Union (NFU)
Agriculture House
Knightsbridge
London SW1X 7NJ
(071) 235 5077

National Federation of Consumer Groups
12 Mosley Street
Newcastle-upon-Tyne
NE1 1DE
(091) 261 8259

National Fruit Variety Collections
Brogdale
Nr Faversham
Kent
Gene bank for varieties of fruit, also does research on new varieties.

National Institute of Agricultural Botany
Huntingdon Road
Cambridge CB3 0LE
(0223) 342234

Parents for Safe Food
Britannia House
32 Galena Road
London W6 0LT
(081) 748 9898

Post Office Users National Council (POUNC)
Waterloo Bridge House
Waterloo Road
London SE1 8UA
(071) 928 9458

Post Office Users Council for Northern Ireland
Chamber of Commerce House
First Floor
22 Great Victoria Street
Belfast BT2 7PU
(0232) 441133

Post Office Users Council for Scotland
45 Waterloo Street
Glasgow G2 6AT
(041) 248 2855

Post Office Users Council for Wales
Caradog House
1 St Andrew's Place
Cardiff CF1 3BE
(0222) 374028

Processors and Growers Research Organisation
Research Station
Great North Road
Thornhaugh
Peterborough PE8 6HJ
(0780) 782585
Research association to improve the growing, harvesting and usage of peas and beans.

SATRA Footwear Technology Centre
SATRA House
Rockingham Road
Kettering
Northants NN16 9JH
(0536) 410000
Evaluates materials and footwear for member companies internationally. Operates an independent footwear testing service in cases of dispute. Also acts as consultants in setting up factories both here and abroad.

Union of Shop, Distributive & Allied Workers (USDAW)
Dilke House
Malet Street
London WC1E 7SA
(071) 580 8641

The Vegan Society
7 Battle Road
St Leonards-on-Sea
East Sussex BN37 7AA
(0424) 427393

The Vegetarian Society
Parkdale
Dunham Road
Altringham
Cheshire WA14 4QG
(061) 928 0793

Women's Nutritional Advisory Service
P.O. Box 268
Hove
East Sussex BN3 1RW
(0273) 771366

Government & Politics

ublications:

od's Parliamentary ompanion (pub. annually od's Parliamentary ompanion Ltd, Hurst reen, East Sussex TN19 ?X, (058086) 310.
ographical directory of embers of both Houses of arliament, election results, arliamentary procedure, vernment departments, lomatic list, royal family and me details on the EC.

ouse of Commons fficial Record (Hansard)
aily record of the proceedings House of Commons' debates.

ouse of Lords Official ecord (pub. HMSO)

'acher's Parliamentary ompanion (pub. quarterly ' A.S. Kerswill Ltd, 113 gh Street, Berkhamsted, erts HP4 2DJ, (0442) '6135).
ndon office:
arliamentary Monitoring ervices, 19 Douglas reet, Westminster SW1P ?A (071) 233 8283 — rrent issue only.
ash/cheque on collection.
formation about the members both Houses of Parliament, e Ministries (address, 'phone mbers and names of portant post-holders), uangos, various public offices, e judiciary, EC, consumer otection groups.

Addresses:

When dealing with government departments you must go through the Press Office.

Association of County Councils
Eaton house
66A Eaton Square
London SW1W 9BH
(071) 235 1200

Association of Metropolitan Authorities
35 Great Smith Street
London SW1P 3BJ
(071) 222 8100

Board of Inland Revenue
Press Office
Somerset House
London WC2R 1LB
(071) 438 6692

Buckingham Palace
Press Office
Buckingham Palace
London SW1A 1AA
(071) 930 4832

Cabinet Office
Press Office
Government Offices
Horse Guards Road
London SW1P 3AQ
(071) 270 6370

Campaign for Freedom of Information
88 Old Street
London EC1V 9AR
(071) 253 2445
Lobby organisation campaigning for the statutory right of access to information; personal, environmental, health and safety, etc.

Campaign for Nuclear Disarmament (CND)
162 Holloway Road
London N7 8DQ
(071) 700 2393

Central Office of Information (COI)
Hercules Road
London SE1 7DU
(071) 928 2345
Government office in charge of advertising in all media within the UK. Also supplies the Foreign & Commonwealth Office with material for British information centres overseas. Film unit.

Conservative & Unionist Central Office
32 Smith Square
London SW1P 3HH
(071) 222 9000

Convention of Scottish Local Authorities
Rosebery House
9 Haymarket Terrace
Edinburgh EH12 5XZ
(031) 346 1222

Council on Tribunals
22 Kingsway
London WC2B 6LE
(071) 936 7045
Keeps under review the constitutions and workings of administrative tribunals and statutory enquiries.

Department for National Savings
Charles House
375 Kensington High Street
London W14 8SD
(071) 605 9483 (PR)

Department of Education & Science
Elizabeth House
York Road
London SE1 7PH
(071) 934 9000

Department of Employment
Caxton House
Tothill Street
London SW1P 9NF
(071) 273 3000

Department of Energy
1 Palace Street
London SW1E 5HE
(071) 238 3000

Department of Health
Richmond House
79 Whitehall
London SW1A 2NS
(071) 210 3000

Department of Social Security
Richmond House
79 Whitehall
London SW1A 2NS
(071) 210 3000

Department of Trade & Industry
Press Office
1 Victoria Street
London SW1H 0ET
(071) 215 5065 ~~5065~~ *5000*
Has a useful library which is
open to the public.

Department of Transport
2 Marsham Street
London SW1P 3EB
(071) 276 0800

Duchy of Cornwall
10 Buckingham Gate
London SW1E 6LA
(071) 834 7346

EC Information Office
8 Storey's Gate
London SW1P 3AT
(071) 222 8122

Fabian Society
11 Dartmouth Street
London SW1H 9BN
(071) 222 8877
Social and political research
(left).

Foreign & Commonwealth Office
HM Diplomatic Service
Downing Street
London SW1A 2AL
(071) 270 3000

Government Actuary's Department
22 Kingsway
London WC2B 6LE
(071) 242 6828

The Green Party
10 Station Parade
Balham High Road
London SW12 9AZ
(081) 673 0045

Hansard Society for Parliamentary Government
16 Gower Street
London WC1E 6DP
(071) 323 1131
Information about the structure
and workings of Parliament.

Her Majesty's Stationery Office (HMSO)
St Crispins
Duke Street
Norwich NR3 1PD
(0603) 622211
Enquiries & bookshop:
High Holborn
London WC1V 6HB
(071) 873 0011
All government publications,
e.g. Acts of Parliament, white
papers, and more general
books from government owned
sources, e.g. designs from the
Victoria & Albert Museum's
collections.

HM Customs & Excise
Clement House
14-18 Gresham Street
London EC2V 7BN
(071) 600 0222

HM Treasury
Information Division
Treasury Chambers
Parliament Street
London SW1P 3AG
(071) 270 3000

Home Office
Queen Anne's Gate
London SW1H 9AT
(071) 273 3000

House of Commons
London SW1A 0AA
(071) 219 4272

House of Lords
Information Office
London SW1A 0PW
(071) 219 3107

Inland Revenue Staff Federation (IRSF)
Douglas Houghton House
231 Vauxhall Bridge Road
London SW1V 1EH
(071) 834 8254

The Labour Party
150 Walworth Road
London SE17 1JT
(071) 701 1234

Liberal Democrats
4 Cowley Street
London SW1P 3NB
071) 222 7999

Local Government Information Unit (LGIU)
2nd Floor
1-5 Bath Street
London EC1V 9QQ
(071) 608 1051
Promotes the case for local
government. 70 local councils
and 8 national trades union are
affiliated.

London Residuary Body
Globe House
4 Temple Place
London SE1 7PB
(071) 633 5000

Ministry of Agriculture, Fisheries & Food
Whitehall Place
London SW1A 2HH
(071) 270 3000

Ministry of Defence
Main Building
Whitehall
London SW1A 2HB
(071) 218 9000

**National Association of
Local Government**
c/o Manchester City Council
Town Hall
Manchesteer M60 2LA
(061) 234 3077

**National Committee for
Electoral Reform**
50 Chandos Place
London WC2N 4BG
(071) 240 1719
Pressure group for the adoption
of proportional representation.

**National Council for Civil
Liberties (NCCL)**
21 Tabard Street
London SE1 4LA
(071) 403 3888

National Peace Council
88 Islington High Street
London W1 8EJ
(071) 354 5200
Umbrella organisation servicing
the peace movement.

**National Union of Civil
and Public Servants**
124-130 Southwark Street
London SE1 OTU
(071) 928 9671

Northern Ireland Office
Whitehall
London SW1A 2AZ
(071) 210 3000

**Ombudsman/Parliament-
ary & Health Service
Commissioner**
Church House
Great Smith Street
London SW1P 3BW
(071) 276 3000

Peace Pledge Union
5 Endsleigh Street
London WC1H 0DX
(071) 387 5501
Pacifist organisation. Runs the
White Poppy Campaign at
Remembrance Sunday.
Campaigns against war toys
and violence on TV.

Plaid Cymru
51 Cathedral Road
Cardiff CF1 9HD
(0222) 231944

Policy Studies Institute
100 Park Village East
London NW1 3SR
(071) 387 2171
Independent research
organisation undertaking work
into economic, industrial and
social policy.

Prime Minister's Office
10 Downing Street
London SW1A 2AA
(071) 930 4433

**Recruitment and
Assessment Services**
(formerly **Civil Service
Commission**)
Alencon Link
Basingstoke
Hants RG21 1JB
(0256) 468551
Recruitment for the Civil
Service.

**Research Institute for the
Study of Conflict and
Terrorism (RISCT)**
136 Baker Street
London W1M 1FH
(071) 224 2659

Royal Mint
Llantrisant
Pontyclun
Mid. Glamorgan CF7 8YT
(0443) 222111

**Scientists Against Nuclear
Arms (SANA)**
9 Poland Street
London N1V 3DG
(071) 734 5281

Scottish Information Office
New St Andrews House
Edinburgh EH1 3TD
(031) 244 1111
Government press office for the
Scottish Office. Also covers
legal matters like the Lord
Advocate, the Crown Office,

Solicitor General for Scotland
and courts administration, also
land registry.

Scottish National Party
6 North Charlotte Street
Edinburgh EH2 4JH
(031) 226 3661

Scottish Office
Dover House
Whitehall
London SW1A 2AU
(071) 270 3000

Training Agency (formerly
MSC)
Moorfoot
Sheffield S1 4PQ
(0742) 753275
Training arm of the Department
of Employment.

**Ulster Democratic
Unionist Party**
296 Albert Bridge Road
Belfast BT5 46X
(0232) 458597

Ulster Unionist Party
3 Glengall Street
Belfast BT12 5AE
(0232) 324601

Welsh Office
Gwydyr House
Whitehall
London SW1A 2ER
(071) 270 3000
Cathay's Park
Cardiff CF1 3NQ
(0222) 825111

Housing

Addresses:
Alone in London
West Lodge
190 Euston Road
London NW1 2EF
(071) 387 5813
Works with young homeless people in London.

Building Employers Confederation
82 New Cavendish Street
London W1M 8AD
(071) 580 5588
At the same address are a number of smaller associations covering specialised aspects of building.

Building Research Establishment
Bucknall's Lane
Garston, Watford
Herts WD2 7JR
(0923) 664664
Government organisation doing research into all aspects of buildings. Work contributes to building regulations. Has a fire research section.

Building Societies Association
3 Saville Row
London W1X 1AF
(071) 437 0655

Campaign for Bedsit Rights
5-15 Cromer Street
London WC1H 8LS
(071) 278 0598

CHAR
5-15 Cromer Street
London WC1H 8LS
(071) 833 2071
Housing campaign for single people.

Federation of Master Builders
14-15 Great James Street
London WC1N 3DP
(071) 242 7583

Georgian Group
37 Spital Square
London E1 6DY
(071) 377 1722
Advisory group on listed buildings.

Homes for Homeless People (formerly **National Cyrenians**)
Smithfield House
Digbeth
Birmingham B5 6BS
(021) 622 1502
Charity providing shelter and housing for the homeless, especially single people.

Institute of Housing
9 White Lion Street
London N1 9XJ
(071) 837 4280

National Federation of Housing Associations
175 Gray's Inn Road
London WC1X 8UP
(071) 278 6571

National Federation of Housing Co-operatives
88 Old Street
London EC1 9AX
(071) 608 2494

National House Building Council (NHBC)
Chiltern Avenue
Amersham
Bucks HP5 5AP
(0494) 434477/
(071) 637 1248 (PR)
Consumer protection body for the house building industry which sets minimum standards of construction, inspects buildings and provides a 10-year warranty.

Ombudsman to Corporate Estate Agents
P.O. Box 1114
Salisbury
Wiltshire SP1 1YQ
(0722) 333306
Administers a voluntary code of conduct for fifteen of the main estate agents in the country.

Priority Estates Project
62 Eden Grove
London N7 8EN
(071) 607 8186
National organisation working with local authorities to provide estate-based housing management and tenant control on unpopular estates.

Royal Institute of British Architects (RIBA)
66 Portland Place
London W1N 4AD
(071) 580 5533

Royal Institution of Chartered Surveyors
12 Great George Street
London SW1P 3AD
(071) 222 7000

9 Manor Drive
Edinburgh EH3 7DN

Alpha House
3 Rosemary Street
Belfast BT1 1QA

Royal Town Planning Institute
26 Portland Place
London W1N 4BE
(071) 636 9107

SHAC
189a Old Brompton Road
London SW5 0AR
(071) 373 7276
Deal with housing problems within the London boroughs. Some research into housing problems, legal advice, etc.

helter
Old Street
ndon EC1V 9HU
71) 253 0202
mpaigning group for the
meless.

TRA
-18 Strutton Ground
ndon SW1P 2HP
71) 222 5844
ganisation which provides
vice and co-ordinates other
anisations working in the
eas of single-person housing,
ecial needs housing and care.

Mungo's Association
7-221 Harrow Road
ndon W2 5XQ
71) 605 9595
arity for the homeless.

ctorian Society
riory Gardens
ndon W4 1TT
31) 994 1019

The Law, Crime & Punishment

Publications:
Halsbury's Statutes, Halsbury's Laws of England, Halsbury's Statutory Instruments, A Concise Summary of English Law (pub. Butterworth & Co.)
A concise summary of English law, including valid precedents.

The Legal 500: the Major Law Firms in England & Wales (pub. Legalease)
Basically a consumer directory of solicitors by region and legal speciality.

Addresses:
Aftermath
P.O. Box 414
Sheffield S1 3UP
(0742) 326166
Support group for the families of serious offenders.

Apex Trust
Tinkers Farm Road
Birmingham B31 1RR
(021) 411 2929
Charity for training and employment services for ex-offenders.

Association of Chief Police Officers (ACPO)
New Scotland Yard
Broadway
London SW1H 0BG
(071) 230 2456
Police Headquarters
Fettes Avenue
Edinburgh EH4 1RB
(031) 311 3131

Association of Personal Injury Lawyers
c/o Pannone Napier
St Peter's House
Hartshead
Sheffield S10 2EL
(0742) 755899

Bar Council
11 South Square
London WC1R 5EL
(071) 242 0082 (Press Office)
Regulatory body for barristers.

British Security Industry Association (BSIA)
Security House
Barbourne Road
Worcester WR1 1RS
(0905) 21464
Trade association representing private security companies.

Campaign Against Pornography & Censorship
P.O. Box 844
London SE5 9QP
(071) 274 3072
Association dedicated to the elimination of pornography but also to the preservation of free speech and freedom of information.

Centre for International Environmental Law
School of Law
Kings College London
Strand
London WC2R 2LS
(071) 352 8123
Set up from 1.10.89 with St Catherine's College, Cambridge, to provide legal assistance to Third World countries and others with ecological problems.

Charter 88
Foundation House
Perserverance Works
38 Kingsland Road
London E2 8DG

Group working for a Bill of Rights in the U.K.

Council for Licensed Conveyancers
Suite 3
Cairngorm House
203 Marsh Wall
London E14 9YT
(071) 537 2953

Crime Concern
Level 8
David Murray John Building
Swindon SN1 1LY
(0793) 514596
National organisation set up to promote local crime prevention.

Criminal Injuries Compensation Board
Wittington House
Off Tottenham Court Road
London WC1E 7LG
(071) 636 9501

Data Protection Registrar
Springfield House
Water Lane
Wilmslow
Cheshire SK9 5AX
(0625) 535711

Department of the Director of Public Prosecutions
4-12 Queen Anne's Gate
London SW1H 9AZ
(071) 273 3000

Howard League for Penal Reform
708 Holloway Road
London N19 3NL
(071) 281 7722

Industrial Injuries Advisory Association
The Adelphi
1-11 John Adam Street
London WC2N 6HT

Institute of Advanced Legal Studies
Charles Clore House
17 Russell Square
London WC1B 5DR
(071) 323 2978
Runs the Public Law Project which provides legal backup for individuals and organisations challenging decisions by government departments, councils and other public bodies.

Institute of Criminology
7 West Road
Cambridge CB3 9DT
(0223) 335360
Teaching and research organisation. Extensive library.

International Bar Association
2 Harewood Place
Hanover Square
London W1R 9HB
(071) 629 1206

International Law Association
Charles Clore House
17 Russell Square
London WC1B 5DR
(071) 323 2978
Campaigning group on human rights and international law in general.

Justice (British Section of the **International Commission of Jurists**)
95a Chancery Lane
London WC2A 1DT
(071) 405 6018
All-party lawyers' association to promote the rule of law and assist in maintaining the highest standards in the administration of justice.

Laboratory of the Government Chemist
Queens Road
Teddington
Middx TW11 0LY
(081) 943 7000

Provides government departments with an analytical and forensic service. Can provide advice on independent experts in areas such as handwriting or will do the work for a fee, themselves. Does not do police forensic work which carried out by the Home Office's Central Forensic Service or local police laboratories.

Law Centres Federation
Duchess House
18 Warren Street
London W1P 5DB
(071) 387 8570

Law Society
113 Chancery Lane
London WC2 1PL
(071) 242 1222

Law Society House
98 Victoria Street
Belfast BT1 3J2
(0232) 231614

26-27 Drumsheugh Gardens
Edinburgh EH3 7YR
(031) 226 7411

Legal Action Group (LAG)
242 Pentonville Road
London N1 9UN
(071) 833 2931

Legal Aid Head Office
Newspaper House
8-16 Great New Street
London EC4A 3BN
(071) 353 7411

Legal Services Ombudsman
22 Oxford Court
Oxford Street
Manchester M23 3WQ
(061) 236 9532
Final appeal for complaints about solicitors, licensed conveyors and barristers after their professional bodies processes have been exhausted.

xis
Bell Yard
ndon WC2A 2JR
71) 404 4097
tabase of tax cases from
75, other cases from 1945
vering all areas of the law.

rd Advocate's
epartment
elden House
Great College Street
ndon SW1P 3SL
71) 276 3000

rd Chancellor's
epartment
evelyan House
Gt Peter Street
ndon SW1P 2BY
71) 210 8500
ministers the High Courts,
wn and county courts and
me tribunals. Appoints
ges, magistrates and JPs.

e Magistrates
ssociation
Fitzroy Square
ndon W1P 6DD
71) 387 2353

etropolitan Police
w Scotland Yard
oadway
ndon SW1H 0BG
71) 230 1212
ntains the Commissioner's
ference Library which
cludes government reports,
graphies, etc. relating to
lice matters and the archives
partment. Both are not
nerally open to the public but
quests to use them will be
nsidered on individual merit.

tional Association for
e Care & Resettlement
Offenders (NACRO)
9 Clapham Road
ndon SW9 0PU
71) 582 6500/**Scottish**
ssociation for the Care &
esettlement of Offenders
ACRO)
Palmerston Place

Edinburgh EH12 5AP
(031) 220 1623/**Northern**
Ireland Association for the
Care & Resettlement of
Offenders (NIACRO)
169 Armagh Road
Belfast BT7 1SQ
(0232) 320157

National Association of
Prison Visitors (NAPV)
46B Hartington Street
Bedford MK41 7RL
(0234) 359763

National Association of
Probation Officers
3-4 Chivalry Road
London SW11 1HT
(071) 223 4887

National Association of
Victim Support Schemes
(NAVSS)
Cranmer House
39 Brixton Road
London SW9 6DZ
(071) 735 9166
Register of local groups helping
the victims of crime.

Parole Board for England
& Wales
Abell House
John Islip Street
London SW1 4LH
(071) 217 3000

Parole Board for Scotland
St Margaret's House
London Road
Edinburgh EH8 7TQ
(031) 244 3427

Police Complaints
Authority
10 Great George Street
London SW1P 3AE
(071) 273 6450

Police Federation of
England & Wales
15-17 Langley Road
Surbiton
Surrey KT6 6LP
(081) 399 2224

Portia Trust
Portia Centre
Maryport Workspace
Solway Trading Estate
Maryport
Cumbria CA15 8NF
(0900) 812114
Voluntary organisation that
counsels and advises people
accused or convicted of
shoplifting.

Prison Officers
Association
Cronin House
245 Church Street
Edmonton
London N9 9HW
(081) 803 0255

Prison Reform Trust
59 Caledonian Road
London N1 9BU
(071) 278 9815/7
Improvement of prisons,
alternatives to prison.

Prisoners Wives &
Families Society
254 Caledonian Road
London N1 0NG
(071) 278 3981
Help and advice for prisoners'
families.

PROP
BM Prop
London WC1N 3XX
(081) 542 3744
Ex-prisoners group concerned
with the welfare of those in
prison.

Rights of Women
52-54 Featherstone Street
London EC1Y 8RT
(071) 251 6577
Advice, information and research on women and the law.

Solicitors Complaints
Bureau
Portland House
Stag Place
London SW1E 5BL
(071) 834 2288

Solicitor-General
9 Buckingham Gate
London SW1E 6JP
(071) 828 7155

**Solicitors Family Law
Association**
24 Croydon Road
Keston
Kent BR2 6EJ
(0689) 850227
Press: Andrew Gerry (Sec.)
(071) 836 8400
Concerned with family law and
finding non-litigious solutions to
legal problems.

Women in Prison
25 Horsell Road
London N5 1XL
(071) 609 8167

**Women in Special
Hospitals and Secure
Psychiatric Units (WISH)**
Cabin T
25 Horsell Road
London N5 1XL
Charity working for women in
Rampton, Broadmoor and
Ashworth Hospitals and secure
psychiatric units.

Locations

Publications:
The Buildings of England
by Nikolaus Pevsner.
County by county guide to
architectural landmarks.
Although updated (series
started in the 50's) buildings
tend to go but a useful starting
point for finding locations.

Gazetteer of England (Two
Volumes) Oliver Mason
(1972 pub. David & Charles)
List of English places with O.S.
References.

**Tables of temperature,
relative humidity,
precipitation & sunshine
for the world.**
Meteorological Office
(HMSO 1980 —
6 Volumes)
Average figures over varying
periods of years from weather
stations throughout the world.

Addresses:
British Tourist Authority
Thames Tower
Blacks Road
London W6 9EL
(081) 846 9000

**Cadw Welsh Historic
Monuments**
Brunel House
2 Fitzalan Road
Cardiff CF2 1UY
(0222) 465511

**The Department of Health
& Social Security**
International Relations
(Health) Branch
Alexander Fleming House
London SE1 6BY
(071) 972 2000

**English Heritage (Historic
Buildings & Monuments
Commission for England)**
23 Saville Row
London W1X 1AB
(071) 973 3000
Preservation of ancient
monuments and historic
buildings in England. Advise
DoE on listing of buildings;
provide funding for repairs to
historic buildings, inc. churches
and rescue archaeology.

Glasgow Tourist Bureau
35-39 St Vincent Street
Glasgow G1 2ER

**Historic Houses
Association**
2 Chester Street
London SW1 7BB
(071) 259 5688
Represents private owners of
historic houses, has a location
index.

Historic Royal Palaces
Apartment 45
Hampton Court Palace
East Molesey
Surrey KT8 9AU
(081) 943 4325

The London Map Centre
22-24 Caxton Street
London SW1H 0QU
(071) 222 2466
Ordnance Survey maps.

Playhouse Theatre
Northumberland Avenue
London WC2N 5DE
(071) 839 4292
Victorian theatre (built 1882)
available during the day and in
the evening according to
performance commitments.

**Royal Commission on
Ancient & Historical
Monuments of Scotland**
54 Melville Street
Edinburgh EH3 7HF
(031) 225 5994

he Sealed Knot Ltd
5 Westhall Road
Varlingham Ferry
L3 9YE
R: Mick Parker
)789) 763980
*Muster Master (Battle
Organiser): Bob Leedham*
)789) 488379
roup which re-stages battles
the English Civil War.

**ociety for the Protection
f Ancient Buildings**
7 Spital Square
ondon E1 6DY
)71) 377 1644
ainly interested in buildings
ior to 1714. Have a technical
ection which advises on
storation techniques, etc.
as a register of period
uildings.

he Visa Shop
haring Cross Shopping
rcade
ondon WC2
)71) 379 0419/ 0376
refer to deal initially with
lephone enquiries. Can
dvise on visa requirements for
l nationalities to any location
t can arrange working visas
r selected countries only. Will
en get the visas for you.

**'ales Tourist
oard/Bwrdd Croeso
ymru**
runel House
Fitzalan Road
ardiff CF2 1UY
222) 499909

**'arship Preservation
ust**
MS Plymouth
inity Pier
illbay Docks
ymouth
752) 229269
MS Plymouth is a type 12
jate, built in 1961, available
a film location.

Medicine,
Health & Safety

Addresses:
Accept
724 Fulham Road
London SW6 2QU
(071) 371 7477
Group to help problem drinkers
by cutting down rather than
teetotalism.

**Action and Research for
Multiple Sclerosis (ARMS)**
4A Chapel Hill
Stansted
Essex CM24 8AG
(0279) 815553

**Action for the Victims of
Medical Accidents**
Bank Chambers
1 London Road
Forest Hill
London SE23 3TP
(081) 291 2793

**Action on Disability and
Development**
23 Lower Keyford
Frome
Somerset
(0373) 73064
Organisation committed to
furthering self-help among
people with disabilities in the
developing countries.

**Action on Smoking and
Health (ASH)**
5-11 Mortimer Street
London W1N 7RH
(071) 637 9843
National charity set up by the
Royal College of Physicians to
publicise the health risks of
smoking.

**Action Research for the
Crippled Child**
Vincent House
North Parade
Horsham
West Sussex RH12 2DA
(0403) 210406

**Alzheimer's Disease
Society**
158-160 Balham High Road
London SW12 9BN
(081) 675 6557/8/9

Alzheimer's Scotland
40 Shandwick Place
Edinburgh EH2 4RT
(031) 225 1453

Alcoholics Anonymous
P.O. Box 1
Stonebow House
Stonebow
York Y01 2NJ
(0904) 644026

**Animal Virus Research
Institute**
Pirbright
Woking
Surrey GU24 0NF
(0483) 232441

**Anthony Nolan Research
Centre**
Royal Free Hospital
Pond Street
London NW3 2QG
(071) 431 5306
Research into tissue-typing for
transplant surgery.

**Arthritis & Rheumatism
Council for Research**
41 Eagle Street
London WC1R 4AR
(071) 405 8572

**Association for All
Speech Impaired Children
(AFASIC)**
347 Central Markets
Smithfield
London EC1A 9LH
(071) 236 3632/6487

Association for Research into Restricted Growth
103 St Thomas Avenue
Hayling Island
Hants PO11 0EU
(0705) 461813

Association for Spina Bifida and Hydrocephalus (ASBAH)
22 Upper Woburn Place
London WC1H 0EP
(071) 252 6325

Association for the Vaccine Damaged Children
2 Church Street
Shipston on Stour
Warwickshire CV36 4AP
(0608) 61595

Association of Community Health Councils
30 Drayton Park
London N5 1PB
(071) 609 8405
National HQ of CHC's which are independent bodies representing the interests of the public in the NHS.

Association of Community Technical Aid Centres Ltd
Royal Institution
Colquitt Street
Liverpool L1 4DE
(051) 708 7607

Association of Medical Research Charities
14-18 Ulster Place
London NW1 5HD
(071) 935 1320

Association of Scottish Local Health Councils
21 Torphichen Street
Edinburgh EH3 8HX
(031) 229 2344

The Asthma Society
300 Upper Street
London N1 2XX
(071) 226 2260

Baby Life Support Systems (BLISS)
17-21 Emerald Street
London WC1N 3QL
(071) 831 9393
Charity formed to buy equipment and services for babies needing intensive medical care.

Blood Products Laboratory
Dagger Lane
Elstree
Herts WD6 3BX
(081) 905 1818
Preparation of blood products used in medical treatments in England and Wales, also research into new methods and products. Preparation of reagents used in the testing of blood and other investigative procedures.

Breast Care & Mastectomy Association
26 Harrison Street
London WC1H 8JG
(071) 837 0908

British Association of Aesthetic Plastic Surgeons
Royal College of Surgeons
35-43 Lincoln's Inn Field
London WC2A 3PN
(071) 636 4864

British Association of Cancer United Patients (BACUP)
121 Charterhouse Street
London EC1M 6AA
(071) 608 1785/6

British Association of the Hard of Hearing
7-11 Armstrong Road
London W3 7JL
(081) 743 1110

British Association of Occupational Therapists
6-8 Marshalsea Road
London SE1 1HL
(071) 357 6480

British Deaf Association
38 Victoria Place
Carlisle CA1 1HU
(0228) 48844

British Dental Association
64 Wimpole Street
London W1M 8AL
(071) 935 0875

British Diabetic Association
10 Queen Anne Street
London W1M 0BD
(071) 323 1531

British Epilepsy Association
Anstey House
40 Hanover Square
Leeds LS3 1BE
(0532) 439393

British Holistic Medical Association
(071) 262 5299

British Kidney Patients Association
Bordon
Hampshire
(0403) 2021/2
Information and support for kidney patients and their families. Operates holiday dialysis centres.

British Medical Association (BMA)
BMA House
Tavistock Square
London WC1H 9JP
(071) 387 4499

British Postgraduate Medical Federation
33 Millman Street
London WC1N 3EJ
(071) 831 6222
Member Institutes: Cancer Research, Child Health, Dental Surgery, Heart & Lung, Neurology, Ophthalmology, Psychiatry, Hunterian.

British Pregnancy Advisory Service
Guildhall Buildings
Navigation Street
Birmingham BT2 4OL
021) 643 1461

British Psychological Society
18 Princess Road East
Leicester LE1 7DR
0533) 549568
Advancement of knowledge
pure and applied) of
psychology.

British Society of Experimental and Clinical Hypnosis
Argyle House
9 Williamson Road
Sheffield S11 9AR
0742) 852222

British Society of Hypnotherapists
37 Orbain Road
London SW6 7JZ
071) 385 1166

British Society of Medical and Dental Hypnosis
42 Links Road
Ashstead
Surrey KT21 2HJ
0372) 273522

British Surgical Trades Association
1 Webbs Court
Buckhurst Avenue
Sevenoaks
Kent
0732) 459225
Trade organisation representing
manufacturers of products for
people with disabilities.

British Union for the Abolition of Vivisection
16A Crane Grove
London N7 8LB
071) 700 4888

BUPA
Provident House
Essex Street
London WC2R 3AX
(071) 353 5212

Cancerlink
17 Britannia Street
London WC1X 9JN
(071) 833 2451

The Centre of Medical Law and Ethics
Kings College
University of London
The Strand
London WC2R 2LS
(071) 836 5454 Extn.1216

Chartered Society of Physiotherapy
14 Bedford Row
London WC1R 4ED
(071) 242 1941

Chest Heart & Stroke Association
CHSA House
123-127 Whitecross Street
London EC1Y 8JJ
(071) 490 7999

Child 2000 (formerly **National Rubella Council)**
311 Gray's Inn Road
London WC1X 8PT
(071) 837 0623
Consortium of 11 national
voluntary organisations
committed to eliminate rubella
(German measles).

Child Accident Prevention Trust
28 Portland Place
London W1N 4DE
(071) 636 2545
Provides information to
professionals on approaches to
accident prevention. Library
open by appointment. Nominal
fee.

Child Growth Foundation
2 Mayfield Avenue
London W4 1PW
(081) 994 7625

Cleft Lip & Palate Association (CLAPA)
1 Eastwood Gardens
Kenton
Newcastle-upon-Tyne
NE3 3DQ
(091) 285 9396

COHSE (Confederation of Health Service Employees)
Glen House
High Street
Banstead
Surrey SM7 2LH
(0737) 353322

College of Dietary Therapy
Hillsborough House
Ashley
Tiverton
Devon EX16 5PA
(0884) 252027
Treatment through diet for
mental and physical problems.

College of Occupational Therapists
20 Rede Place
Off Chepstow Place
London W2 4TW
(071) 229 9738/9

Committee on Safety of Medicines
Market Towers
1 Nine Elms Lane
London SW8 5NQ
(071) 720 2188

The Companion Animal Research Group
Department of Clinic
Veterinary Medicine
307 Huntingdon Road
Cambridge CB3 0JQ
Organisation doing research
into the effects of pet-owning
on the sick.

Council Against Health Fraud
Box CAHF
London WC1N 3XX
(081) 673 4401

Group of campaigners against fraudulent or unverified medical practices and practitioners.

Cystic Fibrosis Research Trust
Alexander House
5 Blyth Road
Bromley
Kent BR1 3RS
(081) 464 7211

The Disability Alliance
1st Floor East
Universal House
88-94 Wentworth Street
London E1 7SA
(071) 247 8776

Disfigurement Guidance Centre
P.O. Box 7
Coupar
Fife KY15 4PF
(0333) 312350

Driving Management Ltd
Audubon House
Bradchutts Lane
Cookham Dene
Berks SL6 9AA
(06285) 27387
Company which runs anti-hijack courses for chauffeurs and those at risk from terrorists/kidnappers. Also runs courses for women to minimise risks of being attacked while driving.

English National Board for Nursing , Midwifery and Health Visiting
Victory House
170 Tottenham Court Road
London W1P 9LG
(071) 388 3131

Environmental Medicine Foundation
Symondsbury House
Bridport
Dorset DT6 6HB
Chair: Lady Colfox
(0308) 22956

Ethnic Switchboard
2B Lessingham Avenue
London SW17 8LU
(081) 682 0216/767 9674
Organisation promoting health care arising from reasons of race, gender, language or culture.

Exploring Parenthood
41 North Road
London N7 9DP
(071) 607 9647
Provides family counselling and telephone advice, also training courses on the needs of children and parents.

EXTEND (Exercise Training for the Elderly and/or Disabled)
1A North Street
Sheringham
Norfolk NR26 8LJ
(0263) 822479

Family Planning Information Service
27-35 Mortimer Street
London W1N 7RJ
(071) 580 2333
Information and statistics on birth control, fertility and relationships.

Fellowship of Depressives Anonymous (FDA)
36 Chestnut Avenue
Beverley
North Humberside
HU17 9QU
(0482) 860619

Foundation for the Study of Infant Deaths
35 Belgrave Square
London SW1X 8QB
(071) 235 1721
Research into the cause of cot deaths.

General Council and Register of Osteopaths
56 London Street
Reading
Berkshire RG1 4SQ
(0734) 576585

General Dental Council
37 Wimpole Street
London W1M 8DQ
(071) 486 2171

General Medical Council
44 Hallam Street
London W1N 6AE
(071) 580 7642

Good Practices in Mental Health
380-384 Harrow Road
London W9 2HU
(071) 289 2034/3060

Haemophilia Society
123 Westminster Bridge Road
London SE1 7HR
(071) 928 2020

Headway (National Head Injuries Association)
7 King Edward Court
King Edward Street
Nottingham NG1 1EW
(0602) 240800

Health Education Authorit
Hamilton House
Mabledon Place
London WC1H 9TX
(071) 383 3833
Responsible for public education on matters of health.

Health & Safety Executive
1-13 Chepstow Place
Westbourne Grove
London W2 4TF
(071) 221 0870
Public body which implements the Health & Safety At Work Ac and related legislation. Regional branches.

The Herpes Association
41 North Road
London N7 9OP

HM Coastguard
Coastguard HQ
Sunley House
90-93 High Holborn
London WC1V 6LP
(071) 405 6911

Hyperactive Children's Support Group
71 Whyke Lane
Chichester
West Sussex PO19 2LD
(0903) 725182

Imperial Cancer Research Fund
P.O. Box 123
Lincoln's Inn Fields
London WC2A 3PX
(071) 242 0200

Institute for Complementary Medicine
21 Portland Place
London WC1N 3AF
(071) 636 9543
Information on alternative medicine and registers of qualified practioners in homeopathy, acupuncture, also herbalists, chiropractors and osteopaths.

Institute of Cancer Research
17A Onslow Gardens
London SW7 3AL
(071) 352 8133

Institute of Child Health
University of London
30 Guilford Street
London WC1N 1EH
(071) 242 9789

Institute of Environmental Health Officers
Chadwick House
Rushton Street
London SE1 0QT
(071) 928 6006

Interim Licensing Authority (ILA)
20 Park Crescent
London W1N 4AL
(071) 600 2705
Monitors clinics offering in vitro fertilisation.

International Federation of Anti-Leprosy Associations
234 Blythe Road
London W14 0HJ
(071) 602 6925

Intractable Pain Society
c/o Dr A.W. Diamond
9 Bedford Square
London WC1 3RA

ISSUE (formerly **National Association for the Childless**)
318 Summer Lane
Birmingham B19 3RL
(021) 359 4887
Advice and information for people with infertility problems.

Karim Centre for Meningitis Research
Queen Charlotte's and Chelsea Hospital
London W6 0XG

King Edward's Hospital Fund for London
14 Palace Court
London W2 4HT
(071) 727 0581

Leukaemia Care Society
P.O. Box 82
Exeter
Devon EX2 5PD
(0392) 64848
Charity providing support for sufferers from leukaemia and allied blood diseases.

London Hazards Centre
308 Gray's Inn Road
London WC1X 8DS
(071) 837 5605
Provide scientific and medical information about safety

hazards at work and in the community.

London School of Hygiene & Tropical Medicine
Keppel Street
London WC1E 7HT
(071) 636 8636

M. E. Association
4A Corringham Road
Stanford-le-Hope
Essex SS17 8EX

Medical Association for Prevention of War
South Bank House
Black Prince Road
London E1 7SJ
(071) 435 1872
Studies the effects of war, both physical and psychological. Concerned with the ethics of doctors vis-à-vis war.

Medical Campaign Against Nuclear Weapons
601 Holloway Road
London N19 4D
(071) 272 2020
Information on the medical and human consequences of nuclear war.

Medical Defence Union Ltd
3 Devonshire Place
London W1N 2EA
(071) 486 6181
World-wide association offering medical indemnity, professional and legal advice to members in the medical industry.

Medical Foundation for the Care of Victims of Torture
96 Grafton Road
London NW5 3EJ
(071) 284 4321
Charity treating the victims of torture, both physical and psychological.

Medical Research Council
20 Park Crescent
London W1N 4AL
(071) 636 5422
Allocates government funds to
medical research projects.

**MENCAP (Royal Society
for Mentally Handicapped
Children and Adults)**
123 Golden Lane
London EC1Y 0RT
(071) 454 0454

**Meningitis Research
Appeal**
Motorways Motel
Alveston
Bristol BS12 2LQ
(0454) 413344

The Meningitis Trust
Fern House
Bath Road
Stroud
Gloucestershire GL5 3TJ

**MIND (National
Association of Mental
Health)**
22 Harley Street
London W1N 2ED
(071) 637 0741

**National Anti-Vivisection
Society Ltd**
261 Goldhawk Road
London W12 9PJ
(081) 846 9777

**National Association for
Health and Exercise
Teachers**
112A Great Russell Street
London WC1B 3NQ
(071) 580 4451

**National Association for
the Welfare of Children in
Hospital**
Argyle House
29-31 Euston Road
London NW1 2SD
(071) 833 2041

15 Smiths Place
Edinburgh EH6 8HT
(031) 553 6553

4 Chestnut Avenue
West Cross
Swansea SA3 4NL
(0792) 404232

**National Association of
Health Authorities**
Birmingham Research Park
Vincent Drive
Birmingham B15 2SQ
(021) 471 4444

**National Association of
Leagues of Hospital
Friends**
2nd Floor
Fairfax House
Causton Road
Colchester
Essex C01 1RJ
(0206) 761 227

National Autistic Society
276 Willesden Lane
London NW2 5RB
(081) 451 1114

**National Back Pain
Association**
Grundy House
31-33 Park Road
Teddington
Middx TW11 0AB
(081) 977 5474

**National Directorate,
National Blood
Transfusion Service**
The N.W. Regional Health
Authority
Gateway House
Piccadilly South
Manchester M60 7LP
(061) 236 2263
Recently established director-
ate overseeing the work of local
blood transfusion centres in
England, Wales and N. Ireland/
**Northern Ireland Blood
Transfusion Service**
89 Durham Street
Belfast BT12 4GE/
(0232) 321414

**Blood Transfusion
Service Board**
Pelican House
40 Mespil Road
Dublin 4
(0001) 603333
Responsible for the work of th
blood transfusion centres in th
whole of Ireland (although
responsibility for press
enquiries for Northern Ireland
also comes under the
directorate in Manchester).
**Scottish National Blood
Transfusion Service**
21 Ellens Glen Road
Edinburgh EH17 7QT
(031) 664 2317/

**National Centre for
Down's Syndrome**
Birmingham Polytechnic
9 Westbourne Road
Birmingham B15 3TN
(021) 454 3126
Advice and research on
children with Down's Syndrom

**National College of
Hypnosis &
Psychotherapy**
12 Cross Street
Nelson
Lancashire BB9 7EN
(0282) 699378

**National Deaf-Blind
League**
Rainbow Court
Paston Ridings
Peterborough PE4 6UP
(0733) 73511

National Eczema Society
Tavistock House East
Tavistock Square
London WC1H 9SR
(071) 388 4097

**National Heart & Lung
Institute**
Brompton Hospital
Dovehouse Street
London SW3 6LY
(071) 352 8121

National Institute for Medical Research
The Ridgeway
Mill Hill
London NW7 1AA
(081) 959 3666

National Organisation for Parents of Visually Handicapped Children
c/o 43 Bettws-y-Coed Road
Cyncoed
Cardiff CF2 6JP
(0222) 752006

National Osteoporosis Society
P.O. Box 10
Radstock
Bath
Avon BA3 3YB
(0761) 32472

National Pharmaceutical Association
40 St Peters Street
St Albans
Herts AL1 3NP
(0727) 832161

National Radiological Protection Board
Chilton
Didcot
Oxon OX11 0RQ
(0235) 831600
Sponsored by Department of Health. Research and advice, sets standards of safe levels in radiation protection.

National Rescue Training Council
The Gatehouse
Hill Head
Llantwit Major
South Glamorgan CF6 9SF
(0446) 792516
Training in water rescue techniques, both sea and inland. Films on lifesaving available.

National Schizophrenia Fellowship
28 Castle Street
Kingston-on-Thames
Surrey KT1 1SS
(081) 547 3937

National Society for Epilepsy
The Chalfont Centre for Epilepsy
Chalfont St Peter
Bucks SL9 0RJ
(02407) 3991
National assessment centre for people with epilepsy. Some research into anti-epileptic medication and psychological aspects. Educational section, up-to-date information on epilepsy.

National Unit for Psychiatric Research & Development
Lewisham Hospital
Lewisham High Street
London SE13 6LH
(081) 690 1184

Nuffield Hospitals
Nuffield House
1-4 The Crescent
Surbiton
Surrey KT6 4BN
(081) 390 1200
Private British hospital group.

Pain Relief Foundation
Walton Hospital
Rice Lane
Liverpool L9 1AE

The Patients' Association
18 Victoria Park Square
London E2 9PF
(081) 981 5676/5695
Information on patients' rights and advice to those with problems in dealing with the health service.

Pesticide Exposure Group of Sufferers (PEGS)
10 Parker Street
Cambridge CB1 1JL
(0223) 64707

Self-help group for those adversely affected by pesticides. Gather evidence about the extent and effect of pesticide exposure on people and environment.

Phobics Society
4 Cheltenham Road
Chorton-cum-Hardy
Manchester M21 1QN
(061) 881 1937

Positively Women
133 Gray's Inn Road
London WC1X 8PX
(071) 837 9705
Organisation providing care and support for women who are HIV+, have AIDS or any related condition.

Princess Margaret Migraine Clinic
Charing Cross Hospital,
Fulham Palace Road
London W6 8RF
(081) 741 7833

Private Patients Plan
PPP House
Upperton Road
Eastbourne
E. Sussex BN21 1BR
(0323) 410505

Psoriasis Association
7 Milton Street
Northampton NN2 7JG
(0604) 711129

Public Health Laboratory Service Board
61 Colindale Avenue
London NW9 5EF
(081) 200 1295

Repetitive Strain Injury Association
Christ Church
Redford
Uxbridge
Middlesex UB8 1SX
(0895) 38663

Research Defence Society
Grosvenor Gardens House
Grosvenor Gardens
London SW1
(071) 828 8745
Organisation to defend the use
of animals in medical
experiments.

**The Retinoblastoma
Society**
National Co-Ordinator
Children's Department
Moorfields Eye Hospital
City Road
London EC1V 2PD
(071) 253 3411
Support group for parents of
children with retinoblastoma, a
tumour affecting the eyes of
babies and children.

RGIT Survival Centre
338 King Street
Aberdeen
Scotland AB2 3 BJ
(0224) 638970

Royal College of Nursing
20 Cavendish Square
London W1M 0AB
(071) 409 2585

**Royal College of
Obstetricians &
Gynaecologists**
27 Sussex Place
London NW1 4RG
(071) 262 5425

**Royal College of
Physicians**
11 St Andrews Place
London NW1 4LE
(071) 935 1174

**Royal College of
Surgeons of England**
35-43 Lincoln's Inn Fields
London WC2A 3PN
(071) 405 3474

**Royal Institute of Public
Health and Hygiene**
28 Portland Place
London W1N 4DE
(071) 580 2731

Royal Life Saving Society
Mountbatten House
Studley
Warwicks B80 7NN
(0527) 853943
Teaches, through local groups
and societies, techniques of life
saving and safety for those
connected with water sports.
General resuscitation methods:
the Kiss of Life people.

**Royal National Institute
for the Blind (RNIB)**
224 Great Portland Street
London W1N 6AA
(071) 388 1266

**Royal National Institute
for the Deaf**
105 Gower Street
London WC1E 6AH
(071) 387 8033

**Royal National Lifeboat
Institution (RNLI)**
West Quay Road
Poole
Dorset BH15 1HZ
(0202) 671133

**Royal Society for the
Prevention of Accidents
(RoSPA)**
Cannon House
Priory Queensway
Birmingham B4 6BS
(021) 200 2461

**Scottish Health Education
Group**
Health Education Centre
Woodburn House
Canaan Lane
Edinburgh EH10 4SG
(031) 447 8044

The Sick Children's Trust
10 Guildford Road
London WC1N 1DT

Charity working to prevent the
separation of parents and
children when a child is gravely
ill in hospital.

Sickle Cell Society
54 Station Road
Harlesden
London NW10 4UA
(081) 961 7795

Society of Chiropodists
53 Welbeck Street
London W1M 7HE
(071) 486 3381

Society of Homoeopaths
2 Arrizan Road
Northampton NN1 4HU

The Spastics Society
12 Park Crescent
London W1N 4EQ
(071) 636 5020

Spinal Injury Association
Newpoint House
76 James's Lane
London N10 3DF
(081) 444 2121

Sports Injuries Centre
National Sports Centre
Crystal Palace
London SE19
(081) 778 0131
Treats all kinds of sports
injuries.

Terrence Higgins Trust
52-54 Gray's Inn Road
London WC1X 8JU
(071) 831 0330
Advice and help for HIV+/AIDS
sufferers.

Thrombosis Research Un
Emmanuel Kaye Building
Manresa Road
London SW3 6LR
(071) 351 8301

Transcendal Meditation
Roydon Hall
East Peckham
Nr Tonbridge
Kent TN12 5NH
(0662) 812671

Voluntary Euthanasia Society
13 Prince of Wales Terrace
London W8 5PG
(071) 937 7770

Women's Nationwide Cancer Control Campaign
Suna House
128-130 Purtain Road
London EC2A 3AR
(071) 729 4688
Helpline (071) 729 2229

Women's Therapy Centre
6 Manor Gardens
London N7 6LA
(071) 263 6200

Overseas

Publications:
Worldwide Government Directory (pub. Cambridge Information Group Directories, Inc., Bethesda, USA)
Addresses and telephone numbers of all government ministries and agencies for every country in the world and international organisations, e.g. UN, EC, WHO, International Court of Justice, Nordic Council, etc.

Addresses:
Amnesty International British Section
99-119 Rosebery Avenue
London EC1R 4RE
(071) 278 6000
Monitors human rights abuse in other countries (Amnesty branches overseas monitor Britain): working for the release of prisoners of conscience; fair and speedy trials for all political prisoners; an end to torture and an end to executions and the death penalty.

Anti-Apartheid Movement
13 Mandela Street
London NW1 0DW
(071) 387 7966

Anti-Slavery International
180 Brixton Road
London SW9 6AT
(071) 582 4040
Charity investigating slavery which, as defined by the UN, now covers debt bondage and exploited child labour in all parts of the world. Only organisation working in this field.

The British Council
10 Spring Gardens
London SW1A 2BN
(071) 930 8466

Promotes British culture and the English language abroad. Maintains lending and reference libraries overseas. Authority on TEFL.

British Overseas Trade Board
1 Victoria Street
London SW1H 0ET
(071) 215 7877

British Red Cross Society
9 Grosvenor Crescent
London SW1X 7E1
(071) 235 5454

Alexandra House
204 Bath Street
Glasgow G2 4HL
(041) 332 9591

87 University Street
Belfast BT7 1HP
(0232) 246 4000

Caribbean Community (CARICOM)
P.O. Box 10827
Georgetown
Guyana
(010) 592 2 69280-89

Catholic Fund for Overseas Development (CAFOD)
2 Romero Close
Stockwell Road
London SW9 9TY
(071) 733 7900

Christian Aid
35 Lower Marsh
London SE1 7RL
(071) 620 4444

Commission of the European Communities
Rue de la Loi 200
1049 Brussels
Belgium
(010 32 2) 234 6111

Commonwealth Institute
Kensington High Street
London W8 6NQ
(071) 602 0702

Commonwealth Secretariat
Marlborough House
Pall Mall
London SW1Y 5HX
(071) 839 3411

Commonwealth Trade Union Council
Congress House
Great Russell Street
London WC1B 3LS
(071) 631 0728
Trade union educational work in developing countries of the Commonwealth.

Consumers in the European Community Group (UK)
24 Tufton Street
London SW1P 3RB
(071) 222 2661

Council for Mutual Economic Assistance (COMECON)
Prospekt Kalinina 56
Moscow 121205
USSR
(010 7 095) 290 9111

Council of Europe
Avenue de l'Europe
F-67006 Strasbourg Cedex
France
(010 33 88) 61 49 61

Court of Auditors
12 rue Alcide de Gasperi
L-1615 Luxembourg
(010 352) 4398-1
EC affiliated organisation.

Crown Agents for Overseas Governments & Administrations
St Nicholas House
St Nicholas Road
Sutton
Surrey SM1 1EL
(081) 643 3311

EC Statistical Office
Bâtiment Jean Monnet
Rue Alcide de Gasperi
L-2920 Luxembourg
(010 352) 43011

Economic Commission for Europe (ECE)
8-14 Avenue de la Paix
Palais des Nations
CH-1211 Geneva 10
Switzerland
(010 41 22) 34 6011
UN regional economic committee

Economic & Social Committee of the European Communities (ECOSOC)
2 rue Ravenstein
B-1000 Brussels
Belgium
(010 32 2) 519 9011

European Centre for the Development of Vocational Training
Bundesallee 22
D-1000 Berlin
Germany
(010 49 30) 884120

European Commission
Audio-Visual Department
Rue de la Loi 200
B-1049 Brussels
Belgium
(010 322) 235 7185
British Media Contact:
Lori Keating
76 Brewer Street
London W1R 3HP
(071) 287 2407

European Commissions (EC)
8 Storey's Gate
London SW1P 3AT
(071) 973 1992

European Court of Justice
Centre Européen
Plateau de Kirchberg
L-2920 Luxembourg
(010 352) 43031

European Foundation for the Improvement of Living and Working Conditions
Loughlinstown House
Shankhill
Co Dublin
01-826888

European Free Trade Association (EFTA)
Information Service
9-11 rue de Varembé
CH-1211 Geneva 20
Switzerland

European Investment Bank
100 Boulevard Konrad Adenauer
L-2950 Luxembourg
(010 352) 4379

European Parliament
Centre Européen
Robert Schumann Building
Plateau de Kirchberg
L-2929 Luxembourg
(010 352) 43001

Institut Français
14 Cromwell Place
London SW7 2JR
(071) 581 2701/589 6211

Institute of Commonwealth Studies
27-28 Russell Square
London WC1B 5DS
(071) 580 5876

Institute of Jewish Affairs
11 Hertford Street
London W1Y 7DX
(071) 491 3517
International research body working on contemporary affairs as they affect the Jewish people.

Institute of Linguists
24A Highbury Grove
London N5 2EA
(071) 359 7445

The Institute of Translation and Interpreting
318a Finchley Road
London NW3 5HT
(071) 794 9931

International Atomic Energy Agency (IAEA)
Vienna International Centre
A-1400 Vienna
Austria
(010 43) 222 2360

International Bank for Reconstruction & Development (World Bank)
1818 H Street NW
Washington DC 20433
USA
(010 1 202) 477 1234

International Court of Justice
Peace Palace
2517 J The Hague
Netherlands
(010 31 70) 92 44 41

International Institute for Strategic Studies
23 Tavistock Street
London WC2E 7NQ
(071) 379 7676
Useful library on international relations.

International Labour Office
Vincent House
Vincent Square
London SW1P 2NB
(071) 828 6401

International Monetary Fund
700 19th Street NW
Washington DC 20431
USA
(010 1 202) 623 7000

International Property Owners Organisation
72 Tottenham Court Road
London W1P 9AP
(071) 323 1225

Local Government Information Bureau
35 Great Smith Street
London SW1P 3BJ
Runs the European Information Service which provides information on the effects of EC policies on local authorities.

Minority Rights Group
29 Craven Street
London WC2N 5NT
International organisation championing the collective rights of minorities.

National Council for the Welfare of Prisoners Abroad
82 Rosebery Avenue
London EC1R 4RR
(071) 833 3467

National Film Board of Canada
P.O. Box 6100
Station A
Montreal
Quebec H3C 3H5
Canada
(010 514) 283 9000

North Atlantic Treaty Organisation (NATO)
Autoroute de Zaventem
B-1110 Brussels
Belgium
(010 32 2) 241 00 40/
241 44 00

Office for Official Publications of the European Communities
2 Rue Mercier
L-2985 Luxembourg
(010 352) 499281

Office of the President
1600 Pennsylvania Avenue NW
Washington DC 20500
USA
(010 1 202) 456 1414

Organisation of the Petroleum Exporting Countries (OPEC)
Obere Donaustrasse 93
A-1020 Vienna
Austria
(010 43 222) 26 55 110

Overseas Development Administration (ODA)
94 Victoria Street
London SW1E 5JL
(071) 917 7000

Oxfam
274 Banbury Road
Oxford OX2 7DZ
(0865) 311311

Royal Commonwealth Society
18 Northumberland Avenue
London WC2N 5BJ
(071) 930 6733

Royal Institute of International Affairs
Chatham House
10 St James' Square
London SW1Y 4LE
(071) 930 2233

The Socialist Group
European Parliament
Rue Belliard 79-113
B1040 Brussels
Belgium

Society for Cultural Relations with the USSR
320 Brixton Road
London SW9 6AB
(071) 274 2282

Third World Information Network (TWIN)
345 Goswell Road
London EC1V 7JT
(071) 837 8222
Two divisions; TWIN & TWIN Trading, which exist to exchange information on trade and technology with the Third World.

The Training Trust
13-14 Ellerslie Industrial
Estate
11 Lyham Road
London SW2 5DZ
Charity to provide training
solutions to individuals and
organisations in developing
countries.

**UK Council for Overseas
Student Affairs (UKCOSA)**
60 Westbourne Grove
London W2 5SH
(071) 229 9268
Represent the needs and
interests of overseas students
studying in this country.

UNAIS
Suite 3A
Hunter House
Goodramgate
York YO1 2LS
(0904) 647799
United Nations agency which
sends project workers overseas
to help with community projects
in agriculture, water supply, etc.

UNESCO
7 Place Fontenoy
75007 Paris
France
(010 331) 45 68 1000

**United Nations
Association of Great
Britain and Northern
Ireland**
3 Whitehall Court
London SW1A 2EL
(071) 930 2931

**United Nations High
Commission for Refugees**
36 Westminster Palace
Gardens
Artillery Row
London SW1P 1RR
(071) 222 3065

**United Nations
Information Office**
Ship House
20 Buckingham Gate
London SW1E 6LB
(071) 630 1981
Reference library of all United
Nations documents, small
information section for general
enquiries. Prefer initial contact
by telephone, although the
library is open to the public.

**United Nations Industry
and Environment Office**
Tour Mirabeau
39-43 Quai André Citröen
75739 Paris Cedex 15
France
(010 33 1) 40 58 88 50

Venice in Peril Fund
24 Rutland Gate
London SW7 1BB
(071) 823 9203

**Voluntary Service
Overseas (VSO)**
317 Putney Bridge Road
London SW15 2PN
(081) 780 2266
Sends skilled volunteers to
work in developing countries on
a wide variety of projects.

War on Want
37 Great Guildford Street
London SE1 0ES
(071) 620 1111

**War Resisters
International**
55 Dawes Street
London SE17 1EL
(071) 703 7189
Pacifist organisation with
international links. Special
interest in conscientious
objectors, monitors individual
cases in other countries.

Womankind
122 Whitechapel High Street
London E1 7PT
(071) 247 6931

Charity providing small loans to
poor women in the Third World
to run their own businesses.

Women Aid
3 Whitehall Court
London SW1A 2EL
(071) 839 1790
Charity, one of whose aims is to
make Third World women
literate.

**Women's Campaign for
Soviet Jewry**
Pannell House
779-781 Finchley Road
London NW11 8DN
(081) 458 7148

**World Health Organisation
(WHO)**
Avenue Appia
CH-1211 Geneva 27
Switzerland
(010 41 22) 91 21 11

People

Parish Registers

From 1538, all churches in England and Wales had to keep a register of baptisms (not births), marriages and burials.

From 1754-July 1837 all marriages had to take place in an Anglican church. Only Jews and Quakers were exempt: they kept their own registers. Non-conformists kept separate baptismal records: some may be at the County Record Office, others with specialist libraries or in the Public Record Office.

Most parish registers are now deposited with the County Record Office, although some may remain at the church. The CRO will tell you their whereabouts.

Publications:

Burke's Peerage
Debrett's
Trade yearbooks of the aristocracy.

The Catholic Directory
(pub. Universe Publications Company Ltd).
List of Roman Catholic clergy in GB plus details of religious societies, schools, colleges, etc.

Contacts (pub. annually by The Spotlight, 7 Leicester Place, London WC2H 7BP (071) 437 7631).
Useful addresses for those in the entertainment industry: agents, theatre and television companies, rehearsal rooms, etc.

Crockford's Clerical Directory
The Who's Who of the Anglican church which lists all clergy and their livings throughout the world.

*Directory of British Associations, (pub. C.B.D. Research Ltd.),
ed. G.P. Henderson & S.P.A. Henderson.
Information on national associations, societies, institutes, etc. with a voluntary membership in all fields: trade, industry, commerce, archaeology, natural history, agriculture, etc.

Dictionary of National Biography (DNB), 22 volumes — (pub. Oxford University Press 1937-38) Additional volumes (9) cover people who died between 1901 & 1980.
Biographies of British historical figures, both well-known and obscure with details of their works, if any, and books about them. As it was last published in the 1930's, no modern material included but a good starting point for biographies and details. Not 100% reliable.

HMSO publish lists of service personnel — serving and retired.

The Minutes of Conference & Directory
(published annually by The Methodist Church).
Methodist ministers and lay people on committees, organisations and offices of the world church.

Self-Help Guide (pub. Chapman & Hall) by Sally Knight and Robert Gann.
List of self-help groups in all fields with addresses and contact numbers.

Showcall (pub. annually by The Stage, Stage House, 47 Bermondsey Street, London SE1 3XT (071) 403 1818).
Directory of singers, entertainers and speciality acts.

Spotlight (pub. annually by The Spotlight, 7 Leicester Place, London WC2H 7BP, (071) 437 7631).
Photographs of actors and actresses (including children) with their agents and/or contact numbers.

Tracing Your Ancestors in the Public Record Office
(HMSO) by Jane Cox & Timothy Padfield (Public Record Office Handbooks No. 19)
Useful for finding information about anyone, not just your ancestors, especially if you want details of someone who was in Government Service, but it is extraordinary what other miscellaneous records the PRO holds, e.g. Prisoners of War, Bankrupts, Victims of Civil Air Crashes, etc.

Addresses:

Army Records Centre
Bourne Avenue
Hayes
Middlesex UB3 1RS
(081) 573 3831
Army records are a nightmare. Serving personnel are held at local centres but this office holds records from the 8th year following discharge of army personnel with no reserve liability. Local record and manning offices carry files before that date and for all serving men who still have reserve liability. Does not hold other ranks or the Guards regiments. Not computerised so all searches made manually according to priority. 1914-1920 held alphabetically but incomplete. 1920 onwards held according to regiment and year of discharge. Will not pass on addresses but will forward letters, if post-1948, via DSS Newcastle who use NI number. Ring first for full details.

College of Arms
Queen Victoria Street
London EC4 4BT
(071) 248 0911 Press Office.
Body consisting of the four Kings of Arms, six Heralds and four Pursuivants who are, under the Earl Marshal, responsible for the ceremonial aspects of state occasions. They are also the regulatory body for granting and controlling armorial bearings.

Court of the Lord Lyon
H.M. New Register House
Edinburgh EH1 3YT
(031) 556 7255
Matters heraldic and aristocratic
in Scotland.

Divorce Registry
Somerset House
Strand
London WC2R 1LP
(071) 936 6000

Judicial Greffe
10 Hill Street
St Helier
Jersey C.I.
(0534) 75472
Wills, probate, adoptions,
divorce, deedpolls, property
registry and register of medical
practitioners in Jersey.

General Register Office
Oxford House
49-55 Chichester Street
Belfast BT1 4HL
(0232) 235211
Records of births and deaths
from 1864 and marriages from
1922. Dublin Record Office
have an all-Ireland marriage
index from 1864 which the
Belfast office will consult on
your behalf and then apply to
the relevant local register office
to obtain a copy certificate.

General Register Office
Custom House
Dublin 1
(0001) 763218

General Register Office
HM New Register House
Edinburgh EH1 3YT
(031) 334 0380
Births, marriages and deaths in
Scotland.

General Registry
Finch Road
Douglas
Isle of Man
(0624) 73358
Holds church records pre-1878
and births, marriages and
deaths since 1878. Also holds
contemporary government
records: ancient records held at
the Manx Museum Library.

Magic Circle
c/o Mr Wilson
29 Shepperton Road
Petts Wood
Kent
(0689) 24676

Naval Secretary's Department
Ministry of Defence
Whitehall
London SW1A 2HB
(071) 218 9000
Initial contact point for enquiries
about senior officers in the
Navy.

Oral History Society
Sec. Dr Robert Perks
c/o National Sound Archive
29 Exhibition Road
London SW7 2AS
(071) 589 6603/4

Principal Probate Registry
Somerset House
Strand
London WC2R 1LP
(071) 936 6000
Wills from January 1858 to
present.

R.A.F. Personnel Management Centre
Eastern Avenue
Barnwood
Gloucester GL4 7AN
(0452) 415181
Records of commissioned
officers, i.e. pilot officers and
above.

R.A.F. Personnel Management Centre
R.A.F. Insworth, P.Man.3.D
Ministry of Defence
Gloucester GL3 1EZ
(0452) 712612
Non-commissioned officers.

Registrar General of Births, Marriages & Deaths
St Catherine's House
10 Kingsway
London WC2B 6JP
(071) 242 0262
All births, marriages and deaths
in England and Wales have had
to be registered here since
1837. Also some registers of
ceremonies conducted abroad
and at sea.

The Registrar-General
Greffe
St Peter Port
Guernsey C.I.
(0481) 25277
Register of births, marriages
and deaths.

The Registrar General
States Office
Royal Square
St Helier
Jersey C.I.
(0534) 77111
Holds records of births, deaths
and marriages from 1842.
Records of Church of England
ceremonies prior to 1842 are
held by the rectors of the
relevant parishes. MS copy of
these early records is held by
the Société Jersiaise.

Royal British Legion
48 Pall Mall
London SW1Y 5JY
(071) 930 8131

New Haig House
Logie Green Road
Edinburgh EH7 4HQ
(031) 557 2782

Royal Marines Association
Central Office
Royal Marines Eastney
Southsea
Portsmouth
Hants PO4 9PP
(0705) 731978
Initial enquiry point for records
of Royal Marines both serving
and discharged.

Scottish Record Office
HM General Register House
2 Princes Street
Edinburgh EH1 3YY
(031) 556 6585

Society of Genealogists
14 Charterhouse Buildings
Goswell Road
London EC1M 7BA
(071) 251 8799
Library open to public on
payment of fee.

Territorial Army
Duke of York's HQ
Chelsea
London SW3 4RY
(071) 730 8131

Public Services & Transport

Addresses:

Air Transport Users Committee
2nd Floor
Kingsway House
103 Kingsway
London WC2B 6QX
(071) 242 3882/3

Associated Society of Locomotive Engineers & Firemen (ASLEF)
9 Arkwright Road
London NW3 6AB
(071) 431 0275

Association of British Wheelclamping Companies
c/o David Humble Associates
Oxbridge House
59 Oxbridge Lane
Stockton-on-Tees TS18 4AP

Automobile Association
Fanum House
Basing View
Basingstoke
Hants RG21 2EA
(0256) 20123

British Airports Authority plc
130 Wilton Road
London SW1V 1LQ
(071) 834 9449
Owns and operates 7 airports in the UK: Heathrow, Gatwick, Stansted, Glasgow, Edinburgh, Prestwick and Aberdeen.

British Coal
(formerly **National Coal Board**)
Hobart House
Grosvenor Place
London SW1X 7AE
(071) 235 2020

British Gas Corporation
59 Bryanston Street
London W1A 2AZ
(071) 723 7030

British Motor Industry Heritage Trust
Castle Road
Studley
Warwickshire B80 7AJ
(0527) 853111
Archive of the British motor industry, also hire out old vehicles.

British Nuclear Forum
22 Buckingham Gate
London SW1E 6LB
(071) 828 0116
'The NEIG was set up by the industry to provide information, answer questions and provide a forum for discussion. Our aim is to widen understanding on the key aspects of nuclear generation of electricity and to put the issues into proper perspective.'

British Ports Federation
Victoria House
Vernon Place
London WC1B 4LL
(071) 242 1200

British Railways Board
Euston House
24 Eversholt Street
London NW1 1DZ
(071) 928 5151

British Telecommunications plc
81 Newgate Street
London EC1A 7AJ
(071) 356 5000

British Telecommunications Unions Committee
14-15 Bridgewater Square
London EC2Y 8BS
(071) 628 4914

British Waterways Board
Graycaine Road
Watford
Herts WD2 4JR
(0923) 226422

Bus and Coach Council
Sardinia House
52 Lincoln's Inn Field
London WC2A 3LZ
(071) 831 7546

Central Transport Consultative Committee
Golden Cross House
Duncannon Street
London WC2N 4JF
(071) 839 7338
British Rail problems, regional committees.

Civil Aviation Authority
CAA House
45-59 Kingsway
London WC2B 6TE
(071) 379 7311
Body responsible for the regulation and control of UK civil aviation.

Dial-a-Ride Users Association
St Margarets
25 Leighton Road
London NW5 2QD
(071) 482 2325

Disabled Drivers Association
Ashwellthorpe
Norwich NR16 1EX
(050) 841 449

Environmental Transport Association
15A George Street
Croydon CRO 1LA

Gas Consumers Council
Abford House
15 Wilton Street
London SW1V 1LT
(071) 931 9151

86 George Street
Edinburgh EH2 3BU
(031) 226 6523

Independent Committee for the Supervision of Standards of Telephone Information Services
67-69 Whitfield Street
London W1P 5RL
(0800) 500212 (public)
(071) 636 6577 (press)

International Air Transport Association (IATA)
Imperial House
15-19 Kingsway
London WC2B 6UN
(071) 240 9036

*Public Information
Department*
P.O. Box 160
1216 Cointrin
Geneva
Switzerland
(010 41 22) 983366
No press office at London
address: all queries to Geneva.
World trade organisation of
scheduled airlines concerned
with air safety and efficiency in
the areas of avionics and
telecommunications,
engineering and environment,
airports, flight operations,
medical and security.

**International Civil Aviation
Organisation**
P.O. Box 400
International Aviation Square
1000 Sherbrooke Street
West
Montreal PQ H3A 2R2
Canada
(010 1 514) 285 8219

Motability
2nd Floor
Gate House
West Gate
Harlow
Essex CM20 1HR
(0279) 635666
Charity which helps disabled
people to buy and hire cars and
with driving lessons.

**National Federation of
Bus Users**
6 Holmhurst Lane
St. Leonards-on-Sea
East Sussex TN37 7LW
(0424) 752424

National Grid plc
National Grid House
Sumner Street
London SE1 9JU
(071) 620 8000

**National Motorcycle
Museum**
Coventry Road
Bickenhill
Solihull
West Midlands B92 0EJ
(06755) 3311

National Postal Museum
King Edward Building
King Edward Street
London EC1A 1LP
(071) 239 5420

National Power
Sudbury House
Paternoster
15 Newgate Street
London EC1A 7AU
(071) 634 5111

**National Union of
Railwaymen (NUR)**
Unity House
Euston Road
London NW1 2BL
(071) 387 4771

Northern Telecom
(formerly **STC plc**
(**Standard Telephones &
Cables**)
Oakley Road
New Southgate
London N11 1HB
(081) 945 4000 - PR Office
Communications and
information systems group:
manufacturers of telephones,
fibre optic cables in underwater
communications. BT is a major
customer.

Nuclear Electricity plc
Barnett Way
Barnwood
Gloucester
Gloucestershire GL4 7RS
(0452) 652222

**Office of Electricity
Regulations**
(formerly **Electricity
Consumers Council**)
11 Belgrave Road
London SW11 1RB
(071) 233 6366

Office of Water Services
Centre City Tower
Seven Hill Street
Birmingham B5 4UA
(021) 625 1300
Consumer watchdog for the
water industry.

Post Office
Royal Mail Headquarters
148-166 Old Street
London EC1V 9HQ
(071) 490 2888

**Post Office Users National
Council (POUNC)**
Waterloo Bridge House
Waterloo Road
London SE1 8UA
(071) 928 9458

**Road Safety Engineering
Laboratory**
Middlesex Polytechnic
The Burroughs
Hendon
London NW4 4BT
(081) 202 6545
Tests prototype seatbelts, child
safety seats and wheelchair
restraints for minibuses.

Sealink Stena Line
Charter House
Park Street
Ashford
Kent TN24 8EX
(0233) 647022

**Steering Developments
Ltd**
Unit 3
Eastman Way
Hemel Hempstead
Herts HP2 7HF
(0442) 212918
Company that assesses needs
and converts vehicles for the
disabled.

Sustrans
37 King Street
Bristol BS1 4DZ
(0272) 268893
A charity which turns disused
railway lines into cycle routes.

**Transport & General
Workers Union (TGWU)**
Transport House
Smith Square
London SW1P 3JB
(071) 828 7788

Trinity House
Tower Hill
London EC3 4DH
(071) 480 6601
General Lighthouse Authority
for England, Wales, CI and
Gibraltar; the main Pilotage
Authority for the UK. Runs the
Charitable Organisation for the
Relief of Mariners.

**United Kingdom Atomic
Energy Authority, (UKAEA)**
11 Charles II Street
London SW1Y 4QP
(071) 930 5454

**Water Services
Association**
1 Queen Anne's Gate
London SW1H 9BT
(071) 222 8111

Religion & Beliefs

Publications:
UK Christian Handbook
(pub. Marc Europe)
Directory of Christian groups in
all areas of work and recreation.

Addresses:
Archbishop of Canterbury
Lambeth Palace
London SE1 7JU
(071) 928 8282

**Association for the
Scientific Study of
Anomalous Phenomena**
St Aldhelm
20 Paul Street
Frome
Somerset BA11 1DX
(0373) 51777
Investigates areas of human
experience and phenomena for
which no generally accepted
explanation yet exists. Library
and archives.

Bible Society
Stonehill Green
Westlea
Swindon
Wiltshire SN5 7DG
(0793) 513713

**Board of Deputies of
British Jews**
Woburn House
Tavistock Square
London WC1H 0EZ
(071) 387 4044
Orthodox and Reform.

**British Council of
Churches**
Inter-Church House
35-41 Lower Marsh
London SE1 7RL
(071) 620 4444
Association of broadly Anglican
Christian churches in the UK
and Republic of Ireland dealing
with community affairs, world
mission, ecumenical and
international affairs.

**British Humanist
Association**
14 Lambs Conduit Pass
London WC1R 4RH
(071) 430 0908

British Youth for Christ
Cleobury Place
Cleobury Mortimer
Kidderminster
Worcestershire DY14 8JG
(0299) 270260

The Buddhist Centre
51 Roman Road
London E2 0HU
(081) 981 1225

Catholic Media Office
23 Kensington Square
London W8 5HN
(071) 938 2583

The Church Army
Winchester House
Independents Road
London SE3 9LG
(081) 318 1226/3916

**Church Commissioners
for England**
1 Millbank
London SW1P 3JZ
(071) 222 7010
Administer the assets of the
Church of England to pay,
house and provide pensions for
the clergy. Also responsible for
pastoral re-organisation and
redundant churches.

**Church of England
General Synod**
Church House
Great Smith Street
London SW1P 3NZ
(071) 222 9011

**Church of Jesus Christ of
Latter Day Saints
(Mormons)**
Hyde Park Chapel
64 Exhibition Road
London SW7 2PA
(071) 589 8561
HQ of the Mormons in Britain.
Also has a microfiche of birth
and marriage records used for
genealogical research.

The Church of Scotland
121 George Street
Edinburgh EH2 4YN
(031) 225 5722/226 3513

**Faculty of Astrological
Studies**
BN 7470
London WC1N 3XX
(071) 700 3586

Federation of Synagogues
9 Greatorex Street
London E1 5NF
(071) 247 4471
Very orthodox.

The Folklore Society
c/o University College
Gower Street
London WC1E 6BT
(071) 387 5894
Collects, records and studies
folklore.

**General Assembly of
Unitarian & Free Christian
Churches**
Essex Hall
Essex Street
London WC2R 3HY
(071) 240 2384
*The General Assembly
Directory* (published regularly)
& *Handbook* give lists of
ministers & churches.

**Inform (Information
Network Focus on
Religious Movements)**
Houghton House
London WC2 2AE
(071) 955 7654
Advice, information and support
to relatives of those involved in
new religious movements or
cults, e.g. Moonies, scientology.

Jehovah's Witnesses
Watch Tower House
The Ridgeway
London NW7 1RN
(081) 906 2211

**Lesbian & Gay Christian
Movement**
Oxford House
Derbyshire Street
London E2 6HG
(071) 739 1249

**London Museum of
Jewish Life**
Sternberg Centre for
Judaism
80 East End Road
London N3 2SY
(081) 349 1143

Collection of objects, photographs, documents and oral history. Publishes research papers.

London Mosque
16 Gressenhall Road
London SW18 5QL
(081) 870 8517/8519
Information about the Muslim faith.

The Lord's Day Observance Society
6 Sherman Road
Bromley
Kent BR1 3JH
(081) 313 0456

Manchester Jewish Museum
190 Cheetham Hill Road
Manchester M8 8LW
(061) 834 9879

Methodist Church Press Office
1 Central Buidlings
London SW1H 9NH
(071) 222 8010

Mixed Marriage Association
Corrymeela House
8 Upper Crescent
Belfast 7
(0232) 325008
Association for mixed Protestant/Catholic marriages.

Movement for the Ordination of Women (MOW)
Napier Hall
Hide Place
Vincent Street
London SW1P 4NJ
(071) 834 2736

The National Death Centre
20 Heber Road
Cricklewood
London NW2 6AA
(081) 208 2853
Forum for ordinary people and professionals to promote a more open attitude to death.

National Secular Society
702 Holloway Road
London N19 3NL
(071) 272 1266
Promotes secular humanism, campaigns against censorship,

religious privilege and indoctrination in schools, etc.

Office of the Chief Rabbi
Adler House
Tavistock Square
London WC1H 9HN
(071) 387 1066

Religious Society of Friends (Quakers)
Friends House
173-177 Euston Road
London NW1 2BJ
(071) 387 3601

Roman Catholic Bishops Conference Secretariat
39 Eccleston Square
London SW1V 1PD
(071) 630 8220

Salvation Army
101 Queen Victoria Street
London EC4
(071) 236 5222

Sikh Cultural Society of GB
88 Mollison Way
Edgware
Middlesex HA8 5QW
(081) 952 1215
Publishes information on Sikh religion and a quarterly magazine.

Society of Psychical Research
1 Adam & Eve Mews
London W8 6UG
(071) 937 8984

Spiritualist Association of Great Britain
33 Belgrave Square
London SW1X 8QB
(071) 235 3351

Theosophical Society
50 Gloucester Place
London W1H 3HJ
(071) 935 9261

United Reformed Church
86 Tavistock Place
London WC1H 9RT
(071) 837 7661

Union of Liberal & Progressive Synagogues
109 Whitfield Street
London W1P 5RP
(071) 580 1663

United Grand Lodge of England
Freemasons' Hall
Great Queen Street
London WC2B 5AZ
(071) 831 9811

Grand Lodge of Scotland of Antient, Free & Accepted Masons
96 George Street
Edinburgh EH2 3DH
(031) 225 5304

United Society for the Propagation of the Gospel (USPG)
Partnership House
157 Waterloo Road
London SE1 8XA
(071) 928 8681
Anglican missionary society which promotes partnership among churches.

Young Mens Christain Association of Great Britain (YMCA)
640 Forest Road
London E17 3DZ
(081) 520 5599

Young Womens Christian Association of Great Britain (YWCA)
Clarendon House
52 Cornmarket Street
Oxford OX1 3EJ
(0865) 726111

cience &
echnology

ddresses:

FRC Institute of Arable
ops Research
othamsted Experimental
ation
arpenden
erts AL5 2JQ
582) 763133

aspects of research on
able crops: fertilisers, plant
netics, viruses, insects and
er pests, etc.

rmingham Gun Barrel
oof House
anbury Street
rmingham B5 5RH
21) 643 3860

sts all weapons offered for
le in the UK unless they carry
valid proof mark from another
untry.

itish Association for the
dvancement of Science
ortress House
Saville Row
ndon W1K 1AB
71) 494 3326

e British Computer
ociety
Mansfield Street
ndon W1M 0BP
71) 637 0471

ofessional body for those
ployed in computer techno-
y concerned with technical,
fessional and ethical
pects of the work. Particular
erest in computer misuse.

itish Plastics Federation
Belgrave Square
ndon SW1X 8PD
71) 235 9483

e Centre for Alternative
chnology
achynlleth
wys
ales SY20 9AZ
554) 702400

hibition centre and
nsultancy on alternative
hnology covering energy,
d, engineering, building and
ycling.

Electrical, Electronic
Telecommunications &
Plumbing Union (EETPU)
Hayes Court
West Common Road
Bromley
Kent BR2 7AU
(081) 462 7755

Institute of Biology
20 Queensberry Place
London SW7 2D2
(071) 581 8333

Institute of Hydrology
Crowmarsh Gifford
Wallingford
Oxon OX10 8BB
(0491) 38800

Institute of Metals
1 Carlton House Terrace
London SW1Y 5DB
(071) 839 4071

Institute of Physics
47 Belgrave Square
London SW1X 8QX
(071) 235 6111

Institution of Chemical
Engineers
12 Gayfere Street
London SW1P 3HP
(071) 222 2681

Institution of Civil
Engineers
1 Great George Street
London SW1P 3AA
(071) 222 7722

Institution of Electrical
Engineers
Savoy Place
London WC2R OBL
(071) 240 1871

Institution of Mechanical
Engineers
1 Birdcage Walk
London SW1H 9JJ
(071) 222 7899

Intermediate Technology
Development Grou Ltd
103-105 Southampton Row
London WC1B 4HH
(071) 436 9761

International Union of
Crystallography
5 Abbey Square
London CH1 2HU

Lock Museum
54 New Road
Willenhall
West Midlands
(0902) 634 542

Media Resource Service
(formerly The Ciba
Foundation)
41 Portland Place
London W1N 4BN
UK enquiries
(071) 631 1634/(071) 580
0100
European enquiries
(071) 323 0938

Provides names and telephone
numbers of specialists who can
give information on medical,
scientific and technological
subjects.

The National Computing
Centre
Oxford Road
Manchester M1 7ED
(061) 228 6333

Trade association.

Royal Commission for the
Exhibition of 1851
Sherfield Building
Imperial College
London SW7 2AZ

The Royal Society
6 Carlton House Terrace
London SW1Y 5AG
(071) 839 5561

Learned society to promote
public awareness and
understanding of science and
technology.

Royal Society of
Chemistry
Thomas Graham House
Science Park
Milton Road
Cambridge CB4 4WF
(0223) 423991

Has a database of business
information on the international
chemical industry.

Society for General
Microbiology
Marlborough House
Basingstoke Road
Spencers Wood
Reading
Berks RG7 1AE
(0734) 885577

Sound

Publications:
Directory of Recorded Sound Resources in the UK, compiled and edited by Lali Weerasinghe (British Library Publications Sales Unit, Boston Spa, Wetherby, West Yorks LS23 7BQ)

The New Grove Dictionary of Music & Musicians (20 volumes), Editor Stanley Sadie (1980 Macmillan).
Biographical and musicological dictionary with list of works and books about subjects.

POMPI (Popular Music Periodicals Index)
Nos.1-2 (Oct'84-Sept'86)
3-4 (Oct'86-Sept'88)
5 (Oct'88-Sept'89) to be published February 1990 (British Library Publications Sales Unit, Boston Spa, Wetherby, West Yorks LS23 7BQ)
Index of articles from periodicals about popular music, including technological developments and the music industry in general.

Addresses:
The Bell Foundry Museum
Freehold Street
Loughborough
Leicestershire LE11 1AR
(0509) 233414
Unique exhibition of bellfounding and bells.

British Academy of Songwriters, Composers and Authors (BASCA)
34 Hanway Street
London W1P 9DE
(071) 436 2261

British Association of Sound Collections
c/o National Sound Archives
29 Exhibition Road
London SW7
(071) 589 6603

BBC Natural History Unit
Broadcasting House
Whiteladies Road
Bristol BS8 2LR
(0272) 732211
Has a sound library, also a list of freelance enthusiasts who might be able to help.

British Music Information Centre
10 Stratford Place
London W1N 9AE
(071) 499 8567
Information on 20th Century British music. Broadly classical in scope, there is a library of some 20,000 scores plus recordings, videos and CD's.

The Composers' Guild of Great Britain
34 Hanway Street
London W1T 9DE
(071) 436 0007
Trade association for music composers.

English Folkdance and Song Society
Cecil Sharpe House
2 Regent's Park Road
London NW1 7AY
(071) 485 2206
Collects and studies material from the British Isles and other English-speaking countries. Library contains music, songs, some information on folklore and customs and a large photograph collection.

Laboratory of Ornithology
Cornell University
159 Sapsucker Woods Road
Ithaca
New York NY 14850
USA
(010 1 607) 254 2473
American bird calls.

National Sound Archive
29 Exhibition Road
London SW7 2AS
(071) 589 6603/4

Performing Right Society Ltd (PRS)
29-33 Berners Street
London W1P 4AA
(071) 580 5544

Sport & Recreation

Publications:
N.B. All sports associations provide yearbooks: the following two are perhaps the best known

Ruffs Guide to the Turf & the Sporting Life Annual (published annually Macdonald & Co.)
Everything about owners, trainers, jockeys, apprentices, breeders, rules of riding, records and, oh yes, horses.

Wisden Cricketers Almanack (pub. annually John Wisden & Co. Ltd)
Details of cricket matches, players batting averages, etc.

Addresses:
Aircraft Owners and Pilot Association
50A Cambridge Street
London SW1V 4QQ
(071) 834 5631

All England Lawn Tennis & Croquet Club
Church Road
Wimbledon
London SW19 5AE
(081) 946 2244

All England Women's Hockey Association
51 High Street
Shrewsbury
Shropshire SY1 1ST
(0743) 233572

All England Women's Lacrosse Association
4 Western Court
Bromley Street
Digbeth
Birmingham B9 4AN
(021) 773 4422

Amateur Boxing Association
Francis House
Francis Street
London SW1P 1DE
(071) 828 8568

**Amateur Fencing
Association**
1 Barrons Gate
33 Rothchild Road
London W4 5HT
(081) 742 3032

**Amateur Rowing
Association**
6 Lower Mall
Hammersmith
London W6 9DJ
(081) 748 3632

**Amateur Swimming
Association**
Harold Fern House
Derby Square
Loughborough
Leicestershire LE11 0AL
(0509) 230431

**The Badminton
Association of England**
National Badminton Centre
Bradwell Road
Loughton Lodge
Milton Keynes
Bucks MK8 9LA
(0908) 568822

**Billiards & Snooker
Control Council**
Kirksdall Road
Leeds LS3 1LT
(0532) 440586

The Boys Brigade
1 Galena Road
London W6 0LT
(081) 741 4001

British Amateur Federation
Edgbaston House
3 Duchess Place
Hagley Road
Edgbaston
Birmingham B16 8NM
(021) 456 4050

**British Amateur
Gymnastics Association**
Holiday Inn
London Heathrow
Suites 035-037
Stockley Road
West Drayton
Middlesex UB7 9NA
(0895) 446683

**British Amateur Rugby
League Association**
West Yorkshire House
4 New North Parade
Huddersfield
West Yorks HD1 5JP
(0484) 544131

**British Amateur Wrestling
Association**
16 Choir Street
Low Broughton
Salford M7 9ZD
(061) 832 9209

British Athletic Federation
Edgbaston House
3 Duchess Place
Hagley Road
Edgbaston
Birmingham B16 8NM
(021) 456 4050

**The British Ballet
Organisation**
39 Lonsdale Road
London SW13 9JP
(081) 748 1241
Examination and training body.

**British Boxing Board of
Control**
70 Vauxhall Bridge Road
London SW1V 2RP
(071) 828 2133

British Canoe Union
The John Dudderidge House
Adbolton Lane
West Bridgford
Nottingham NG2 5AS
(0602) 821100

British Chess Federation
9A Grand Parade
St. Leonards-on-Sea
East Sussex TN38 0DD
(0424) 442500

**British Crown Green
Bowling Association**
14 Leighton Avenue
Maghull
Liverpool L31 0AH
(051) 526 8367

British Cycling Federation
36 Rockingham Road
Kettering
Northants NN16 8HG
(0536) 412211

British Darts Organisation
2 Pages Lane
Muswell Hill
London N10 1PS
(081) 883 5544

**British Drag Racing
Association**
27 James Street
London W1M 5HY
(071) 486 7676

**British Field Sports
Society**
59 Kennington Road
London SE1 7PZ
(071) 928 4742

**British Hang Gliding
Association**
Cranfield Airfield
Cranfield
Bedfordshire MK43 0YR
(0234) 751688

**The British Horse
Society/Pony Club of
Great Britain**
British Equestrian Centre
Stoneleigh
Warwickshire CV8 2LR
(0203) 696697

**British Ice Hockey
Association**
2nd Floor Suite
517 Christchurch Road
Boscombe
Bournemouth BH1 4AG
(0202) 303946

British Judo Council
1A Horn Lane
Acton
London W3 9NJ
(081) 992 9454

**British Mountaineering
Council**
Crawford House
Precinct Centre
Booth Street East
Manchester M13 9RZ
(061) 273 5835

**British Parachute
Association**
Kimberley House
47 Vaughan Way
Leicester LE1 4SG
(0533) 519778

The British Sports Association for the Disabled
34 Osnaburgh Street
London NW1 3ND
(071) 383 7277

British Sub-Aqua Club
Telford Quay
Ellesmere Port
South Wirral L65 4FY
(051) 357 1951

British Waterski Federation
390 City Road
London EC1V 2QA
(071) 833 2855

The Croquet Association
Hurlingham Club
Ranelagh Gardens
London SW6 3PR
(071) 736 3148

Disabled Drivers' Motor Club Ltd
Cottingham Way
Thrapston
Northants NN14 4PL
(0801) 24724

English Amateur Dancers Association
14 Oxford Street
London W1N 0HL
(071) 636 0851

English Basketball Association
48 Bradford Road
Leeds LS28 6DF
(0532) 361166

English Curling Association
66 Preston Old Road
Freckleton
Preston
Lancs PR4 1PD
(0772) 634154

English Volleyball Association
27 South Road
West Bridgford
Nottingham NG2 7AG
(0602) 816324

The Football Association
16 Lancaster Gate
London W2 3LW
(071) 262 4542

Gaming Board for Great Britain
Berkshire House
168-173 High Holborn
London WC1V 7AA
(071) 240 0821

The Girls' Brigade National Council for England and Wales
Brigade House
Foxall Road
Didcot
Oxon OX11 7BQ
(0235) 510425

The Guides Association
17-19 Buckingham Palace Road
London SW1W 0PP
(071) 834 6242

The Hockey Association
Northdown Street
London N1 9BG
(071) 873 8878

International Table Tennis Federation
53 London Road
St Leonards-on-Sea
East Sussex TN37 6AY
(0424) 721414

The Jockey Club
42 Portman Square
London W1H 0EN
(071) 486 4921
At same address:
National Trainers Federation
Racehorse Owners Association

Lawn Tennis Association
The Queen's Club
London W14 9EG
(071) 381 5965

League Against Cruel Sports
83-87 Union Street
London SE1 1SG
(071) 407 0979

Martial Arts Commission
Broadway House
15-16 Deptford Broadway
London SE8 4PE
(081) 691 3433

Marylebone Cricket Club
Lords Cricket Ground
London NW8 8QN
(071) 289 1611

Modern Pentathlon Association of Great Britain
Wessex House
Silchester Road
Tadley
Hants RG26 6PX
(0734) 810111

Morris Ring
21 Eccles Road
Ipswich
Suffolk IP2 9RG
(0473) 682540
Association of male Morris clubs, also archive including photographs.

National Council of YMCAs
640 Forest Road
London E17 3DZ
(081) 520 5599

National Cricket Association
Lord's Cricket Ground
London NW8 8QN
(071) 289 6098

National Federation of Anglers
Halliday House
2 Wilson Street
Derby DE1 1PG
(0332) 362000

National Greyhound Racing Club Ltd
24-28 Oval Road
London NW1 7DA
(071) 267 9256

National Horseracing Museum
99 High Street
Newmarket
Suffolk CB8 8JL
(0638) 667333

National Playing Fields Association (NPFA)
25 Ovington Square
London SW3 1LQ
(071) 584 6445

National Rifle Association
Bisley Camp
Brookwood
Woking
Surrey GU24 0PB
(0483) 797777

National Skating Association of Great Britain
15-27 Gee Street
London EC1V 3RE
(071) 253 3824

Professional Footballers Association
2 Oxford Court
Bishopsgate
Manchester M2 3WQ
(061) 236 0575

Riding for the Disabled Association (RDA)
Avenue R
National Agricultural Centre
Kenilworth
Warwickshire CV8 2LY
(0203) 696510

Royal and Ancient Golf Club of St Andrews
St Andrews
Fife
Scotland KY16 9JD
(0334) 72112

RAC Motor Sports Association Ltd
Motor Sports House
Riverside Park
Colnbrook
Slough
Berks SL3 0HG
(0753) 681736
Governing body for the UK.

Royal Yachting Association
RYA House
Romsey Road
East Leigh
Hants SO5 4YA
(0703) 629962

The Rugby Football League
180 Chapeltown Road
Leeds LS7 4HT
(0532) 624637

The Rugby Football Union
Rugby Road
Twickenham
Middlesex TW1 1DX
(081) 892 8161

Scottish Youth Hostels Association
11 Woodlands Terrace
Glasgow G3 6DD
(041) 332 3004

Scouts Association
Baden-Powell House
Queen's Gate
London SW7 5JS
(071) 584 7030

Sports Aid Foundation
16 Upper Woburn Place
London WC1H 0QN
(071) 387 9380

The Sports Council
16 Upper Woburn Place
London WC1H 0QP
(071) 388 1277
Has a comprehensive list of the governing bodies of all sports.

Sports Council
Caledonian House
South Dial
Edinburgh EH12 9DQ
(031) 317 7200

Sports Council for Northern Ireland
House of Sport
Upper Malone Road
Belfast BT9 5LA
(0232) 661222

Sports Council for Wales
National Sports Centre for Wales
Sophia Gardens
Cardiff CF1 9SW
(0222) 397571

Tennis & Rackets Association
c/o Queen's Club
Palliser Road
London W14 9EQ
(071) 381 4746

Women's Cricket Association
41 St Michael's Lane
Headingley
Leeds LS6 3BR
(0532) 742398

The Woodcraft Folk
13 Ritherdon Road
London SW17 8QE
(071) 672 6031
Co-educational association for young people from 6-20.

Youth Clubs UK
Keswick House
30 Peacock Lane
Leicester LE1 5NY
(0533) 629514

Visuals

Publications:

The Broadcast Production Guide (pub. International Thomson, 100 Avenue Road, London NW3 3TP (071) 935 6611)
Lists facility houses, production companies, distribution companies, suppliers and manufacturers of equipment, music services, and other specialist services.

Catalogue of Colour Reproductions of Paintings
(Volume 1, before 1860; Volume 2, 1860-1961), (pub. UNESCO, Paris)
Black and white reproductions of works of art with publishers of colour reproductions.

*Halliwell's Film Guide
(6th Edition, pub. 1987 Grafton) by Leslie Halliwell

Halliwell's Television Companion (3rd Edition, pub. 1986 Granada) by Leslie Halliwell with Philip Purser
Covers television programmes in the UK and USA, but omits news, current affairs and sport.

The Knowledge (pub. The PA Publishing Company Ltd, Unit 3, Grand Union Centre, West Row, London W10 5AS, (081) 969 5777).
Directory of contacts in the film/tv industry. Ancillary production services and staff, animal trainers, pilots, graphics, animation, etc.

*Picture Researcher's Handbook (3rd Edition, 1986 Van Nostrand Reinhold (UK) Co Ltd) by Hilary and Mary Evans.
Comprehensive guide to picture libraries in both the UK & abroad. The 2nd edition has useful information on copyright, credits, etc.

*Researcher's Guide to British Film & Television Collections Ed. Elizabeth Oliver, (pub. British Universities Film & Video Council, 55 Greek Street, London W1V 5LR, (071) 734 3687).

Newspapers have photograph libraries and will sell prints of their stills, if they were taken by staff photographers.

Addresses:

British Association of Picture Libraries & Agencies (BAPLA)
13 Woodberry Crescent
London N10 1PJ
(081) 883 2531

BBC Enterprises Ltd
Woodlands
80 Wood Lane
London W12 0TT
(081) 743 5588
Requests to use BBC facilities and some BBC material.

BBC Enterprises Library Sales
Room S142
Reynard Mills
Windmill Road
Brentford
Middlesex TW8 9NF
(081) 758 8444

BBC Enterprises Photograph Sales
Unit 1
29 North Acton Road
Harlesden
London NW10 6PE
(081) 743 8000
Provides photographs taken from radio and TV programmes that have been transmitted from 1935 to the present day.

British Film Institute
21 Stephen Street
London W1P 1PL
(071) 255 1444

British Video Association
22 Poland Street
London W1V 3DD
(071) 437 5722
Trade association for the video industry. Can tell you what is available on video for sale or hire.

East Anglia Film Archive
University of East Anglia
Norwich NR4 7TJ
(0603) 592664
Large archive of film relating to life and work in Norfolk, Suffolk, Essex and Cambridgeshire including much material on farming and rural life.

International Federation of Film Archives (FIAF)
Coudenberg 70
1000 Brussels
Belgium
(010 32 2) 511 1390
Only archives which have a certain standard of storage etc. are admitted as members, so it is not an exhaustive list of overseas film archives. Useful as a starting point, though.

National Aeronautical & Space Administration (NASA)
Washington DC 20546
USA
(010 1 202) 453 8400
Stills and film from space projects.

National Film Archive
21 Stephen Street
London W1P 1PL
(071) 255 1444
In addition to films has an extensive stills library.

National Portrait Gallery/Archive & Library
The Mill
72 Molesworth Street
London SE13 7EW
(081) 318 2888
Appointment only. Archive of British portraits and over 100,000 photographs of distinguished, though not necessarily famous, Britons, e.g. senior civil servants.

National Railway Museum
Leeman Road
York YO2 4X
(0904) 621261
Holds the picture archive (photographs from the early days and posters from 1920s) of British Rail. Not completely catalogued and about 6 weeks delay in producing material at present.

The Post Office Film and Video Group
33 Grosvenor Place
London SW1X 1PX
(071) 245 7703/7862
Has a lot of early documentary material, mostly about the Post Office, but some wartime footage

Remember When
368 Brighton Road
South Croydon
Surrey CR2 6AL
(081) 688 6323
Back numbers of national newspapers from 1640s onwards. A few magazines.

Royal College of Music
Department of Portraits
Prince Consort Road
London SW7 2BS
(071) 589 3643
Collection of portraits of musicians and the largest archive of concert programmes on Great Britain.

Royal Photographic Society
The Octagon
Milsom Street
Bath BA1 1DN
(0225) 462841
HQ of oldest photographic society in the world. 5 galleries house exhibitions; there is also an extensive archive.

SSVC (Services Sound & Vision Corporation)
Chalfont Grove
Narcot Lane
Gerrards Cross
Bucks SL9 8TN
(02407) 4461
Has an archive of military training films including footage of weapons. Much of the material is restricted, but worth trying if you need footage of a particular military weapon.

Welsh Industrial & Maritime Museum
Bute Street
Cardiff CF1 6AN
(0222) 481919
Covers all aspects of Welsh industrial and maritime history, also holds the part of the GWR negative collection covering Welsh railways.